"Luis Palau is an evangelist to three
— *Christianity*

"The strength of Palau's message...can
—*Time*

"Palau...believes fundamental answers to all of life's problems are in the Bible. 'Every new immigrant to the United States needs to be confronted with the claims of Christ.'"
—*Los Angeles Times*

"Evangelist Luis Palau, a naturalized U.S. citizen who was born in Argentina, ranks second behind the Rev. Billy Graham in the number of crusades he has held and is considered by some religious leaders as the heir apparent to Mr. Graham's legacy."
—*Dallas Morning News*

"There are many practical reasons for supporting the ministry of Luis Palau: his fidelity to the truth, his constancy of passion for the lost, and his integrity in personal life—these are sufficient to begin. But the all-encompassing fact that compels my belief in Luis and the outreach of the Palau Evangelistic Association is the evidence of God's sovereign choice to anoint and use this man mightily at this crucial juncture in church history."
—*Jack W. Hayford*
Senior Pastor
The Church On The Way
Van Nuys, California

"As an evangelist, he is second only to Billy Graham."
—*British Broadcasting Corporation*

"The impact . . . of Billy Graham and Luis Palau will be felt for generations to come."
—*Religious News Service*

"Luis Palau is one of God's most gifted evangelists in the world today, and a man for whom I have the greatest possible love and respect."
—*Billy Graham*
Evangelist

"I believe that the best days of citywide crusade evangelism are yet ahead. Luis Palau has the anointing of God to help lead us into these days."

—*C. Peter Wagner*
Professor of Church Growth
Fuller Theological Seminary

"I consider Luis Palau and the Luis Palau Evangelistic Association to be one of the vital forces in world evangelization today. I have been particularly impressed with their concern for wise stewardship of all of the resources entrusted to them. The world needs more examples of men like Luis who with boldness and integrity communicate the truth of the Gospel of Jesus Christ."

—*Ronald W. Blue*
Managing Partner
Ronald Blue & Co.

"I am so encouraged by the Palau Association's emphasis on pre-crusade prayer and the power of God. I had the privilege of training Christians in prayer and intercession for the Luis Palau and Billy Graham crusades in England...the results were incredible. Prayer is the strength of Luis Palau."

—*Evelyn Christenson*
United Prayer Ministries

"I warmly commend Luis Palau as an evangelist of integrity, relevance, and compassion. Luis preaches the biblical Gospel that not only makes people holy and good, but also has an impact on society and community care."

—*The Most Rev. George Carey*
Archbishop of Canterbury
Church of England (Anglican)

"I have the highest regard for Luis Palau and his ministry. His commitment to living the Gospel as well as evangelism is a worthy model of mission. With more young people in the world than ever before, and urban areas worldwide experiencing explosive growth, Luis' ministry is needed more than ever."

—*Rev. Glandion Carney*
Director
InterVarsity Missions Fellowship

LUIS PALAU
CALLING
AMERICA AND
THE NATIONS
TO CHRIST

with David Sanford

THOMAS NELSON PUBLISHERS
Nashville • Atlanta • London • Vancouver

Published in Nashville, Tennessee, by Thomas Nelson, Inc., Publishers.

All references are from the *Holy Bible: New International Version*, copyright 1973, 1978, 1984 by the International Bible Society. Used by permission of Zondervan Bible Publishers.

Scripture references marked NKJV are from *The Bible: The New King James Version*, copyright 1984 by Thomas Nelson, Inc.

Scripture references marked TLB are from *The Living Bible*, copyright 1971 by Tyndale House Publishers, Wheaton, Ill. Used by permission.

Scripture references marked RSV are from the *Revised Standard Version of the Bible*, copyright 1946, 1952, 1971, 1973, Division of Christian Education, National Council of Churches of Christ in the USA.

Library of Congress Cataloging-in-Publication Data
Palau, Luis, 1934-
    Luis Palau : calling America and the nations to Christ / Luis Palau with David Sanford.
        p.   cm.
    ISBN 0-7852-7984-9 (pbk.)
    1. Palau, Luis, 1934- . 2. Evangelists—Latin America—Biography. 3. Evangelist—United States—Biography. I. Sanford, David (David R.) II. Title: Calling America and the nations to Christ.
BV3785.P32A3 1994
269'.2'092—dc20
[B]   94-21741
                                                      CIP

                Printed in the United States of America
                1 2 3 4 5 6 7 8 9 —00 99 98 97 96 95 94

Dedication

I dedicate this book to the glory of God, with thanksgiving for the life-changing power of His Gospel. It's my privilege to be just one of Jesus Christ's ambassadors to America and the nations.

I also dedicate this book to my wife, Patricia; to my four sons, Kevin, Keith, Andrew, and Steve; to my extended family and friends; and to the more than 100 staff members and alumni of the Luis Palau Evangelistic Association—without you, there wouldn't be much of a story.

"We shall have all eternity
in which to celebrate our victories,
but we have only one swift hour
before the sunset in which
to win the lost to Christ."

—*Robert Moffat*

Introduction

Who is this man, Luis Palau? Why are so many people saying such enthusiastic things about him? And what are all these reports about his passion and burden to help re-evangelize America in our day?

Perhaps you've been following Luis Palau's international ministry with interest for years. Or perhaps you've only recently heard about him for the first time.

Luis Palau finally is becoming better known in his adopted homeland, America. His popularity over the years in Latin America, the United Kingdom, and other parts of the world is rather remarkable.

During one crusade, more than 518,000 people in London turned out to hear Luis Palau in person. He so captured the imagination of the British press that it started using his name as a synonym for enthusiasm. A massive, mind-boggling crowd of 700,000 people gathered to hear Luis on Thanksgiving Sunday in Guatemala City a few years ago.

Not that everyone has applauded Luis each step of the way. He has survived death threats and blistering verbal attacks from critics opposed to the ministry of evangelism to the masses.

Yet when all is said and done, Luis Palau stands out in this generation as a truly international Christian spokesman and leader. He's a third generation transplanted European who grew up in the province of Buenos Aires, Argentina, and then chose to become an American citizen after completing the graduate course at Multnomah Biblical Seminary in Portland, Oregon.

Equally at ease in English and Spanish, Luis Palau commands audiences' attention wherever he goes. His solidly biblical, practical messages hit home in the minds and hearts of listeners.

"Sometimes it seems I have been preaching all my life," says Luis. "Actually, although I started preaching in Argentina as a teenager, it really wasn't until I was in my thirties that God opened the door for me to pursue full-time mass evangelism."

During the 1970s, Luis and his team conducted evangelistic crusades and rallies throughout Latin America, leading presidents and peasants alike to commit their lives to Jesus Christ. Invitations also started coming from Europe and other parts of the world. By the early 1980s, Luis Palau's ministry had taken Britain by storm and new doors were opening all around the globe.

Since then, huge crowds in countries as diverse as Brazil and

Colombia, Costa Rica and Denmark, Guatemala and Hungary, Hong Kong and India, Indonesia and Japan, Mexico and New Zealand, Peru and Romania, Russia and Singapore, Thailand and the United States have packed out concert halls, arenas, and stadiums to hear the Gospel preached by Luis Palau. The impact? Hundreds of thousands of people have trusted Jesus Christ and become established as disciples in local churches. Cities and nations have heard a clear-cut proclamation of the Gospel.

"Luis is probably more in demand among evangelicals to preach and speak than almost any other person in the world," says Billy Graham. "Wherever there is an evangelical conference they try to get Luis Palau, because he is a powerful preacher. But more than that, he is an evangelist that God has given a multiplicity of gifts to, and thousands of people come to hear him every year, and other thousands are won to Christ."

Luis Palau has proclaimed the Good News of Jesus Christ to hundreds of millions of people via radio and television in ninety-five nations, and face-to-face to more than 11 million people on six continents.

In addition to his dynamic speaking ministry, Luis Palau is a prolific author. His three dozen books and booklets include the powerful *What Is a Real Christian?* evangelistic booklet, which has been published in thirty-one languages worldwide. Luis also has contributed articles to more than a dozen and a half books and scores of periodicals.

Luis and his wife, Pat, also a popular conference speaker and author, have served as missionary-evangelists in Costa Rica, Colombia, and Mexico. The Palaus have four grown sons and now make their home in Portland, Oregon, near the international headquarters of the Luis Palau Evangelistic Association.

This is Luis Palau's story as it's told best, in his own words. You'll find him refreshingly honest and straightforward. His wholehearted commitment to the Lord and passion to call people in America back to Jesus Christ is inspiring.

Get to know this man, pray for him, and do all you can to support his efforts to help re-evangelize America. Many of the choicest Christian leaders in this nation consider Luis Palau to be God's man for this crucial hour.

—DAVID SANFORD

1

If you watched NBC's broadcast of the gymnastics and volleyball competitions during the summer Olympics in Barcelona, Spain, you've seen what's called the Palau Sant Jordi stadium. My surname, Palau, originated there in Spain, brought to Argentina by my paternal grandfather years ago.

Like many other Americans, the story of my family heritage goes back to Europe, in my case sometime during the twelfth century. Fair-haired Germans invaded northeast Spain, leaving behind something of a legacy. People sometimes express amazement that my sons have blond hair. So did their grandfather and many of their great-grandfathers back through the centuries.

I was born and raised in Argentina, the first grandson of emigrants who sailed over from Spain on my father's side and from Scotland and France on my mother's side. So while I'm from Latin America, culturally I'm just as much from Europe, as are nearly ninety-seven percent of Argentina's sons and daughters.

I'm a Russian salad, in many ways. I was born about as multicultural as you can get, which has given me a unique vantage point from which to identify with many diverse audiences. My religious heritage is quite blended, as well.

My grandparents had little time for religion, except for my maternal grandmother, who was devoted to the French Roman Catholic Church and then made a personal commitment to Jesus Christ as Savior and Lord later in life. My grandfather's parents were from England and Scotland. Although he was officially raised in the Church of Scotland, he preferred to say he was "Scotch Presbyterian." In any case, he should have brought the Gospel with him to Argentina. Instead, although he wasn't a heavy drinker, he definitely preferred Scotch to Presbyterian, and died hours after telling me, one last time, he had a religious upbringing and didn't need to make a personal decision for Jesus Christ. My father's parents were nominally religious, as well.

My parents, Luis and Matilde Palau, like most Argentines in their day, belonged to the state church. I was born November 27, 1934, and baptized into the Catholic church, christened Luis Palau, Jr. Not that the traditional church meant very much to my father. Churches with an evangelistic perspective, on the other hand, were almost a non-entity in much of Latin America in his day.

Through the witness of a British tentmaker missionary, Edward Rogers, an executive with the Shell Oil Company, my mother and then my father trusted Jesus Christ for salvation, entering into a personal relationship with God after an intensive search.

Overnight, my father, a well-to-do businessman who had his own construction company, became an active and bold member of what was then a despised minority of Argentians. Only later, as a boy accompanying my father on evangelistic forays in town and out in the countryside, did I begin to realize how much grief he endured to proclaim what he and the early Christians called "good news!" That news was often greeted with insults, derision, stones, and worse.

Later, in the 1960s, the persecution would subside for the most part, after Pope John XXIII and Vatican II stressed the importance of the Bible and stated that those outside the Catholic church no longer were heretics but simply "separated brethren." Marxist-Leninist forces, however, soon proved to be a much more serious threat, infiltrating some churches and undermining the proclamation of the Gospel.

Our family lived in the small riverside resort town of Ingeniero-Maschwitz, in the province of Buenos Aires. At first there was only a Catholic church, empty most of the time as no priest lived nearby, as I remember it. After my father's conversion, he helped Mr. Rogers build a small Christian Brethren chapel. Today the chapel is still a vibrant center of worship with a nice addition in front of the original building. But most of the people with whom I grew up, except Henry Martin, have since moved south to the capital city or beyond.

A world of change

My world, our world, has undergone massive changes in the past generation and a half. The revolutions haven't been only political. Half of Latin America is now urbanized. Fully eleven percent, including my siblings and myself, have come to personal faith in Christ. And many are now spreading the Gospel abroad, doing their part to help fulfill Jesus Christ's Great Commission to "Go into all the world and preach the good news to all creation" (Mark 16:15).

My father was my hero as a boy. His pride in the Gospel and boldness to share it with others marked my life. After hearing him preach so often, I began imitating his gestures, his voice, and even his words. Actually, I got quite good at it! Maybe that's why I thoroughly enjoyed playing "church" with my little sisters. They had to listen to me preach, like it or not, because I was the oldest. As if they didn't get enough when they were little, two of my sisters, Matilde and Ketty (and her husband, Eric Green), now voluntarily serve the Lord full-time as part of the Luis Palau Evangelistic Association.

According to my mother, when I was three or four years old I knelt beside her as she was praying for us. I heard her say, "Lord, I pray that Luisito will truly come to know You."

I looked at her and said, "But Mommy, I do know the Lord Jesus." I did, in my own way. I did not know Him in a *personal* way until later, but my parents had taught me about God's love and had given me over to the Lord, praying that I would become a faithful servant of the Gospel.

When my parents dedicated me to the Lord, they said: "Lord, here is Luisito. He is Yours. Use him for Your glory and as You wish so many may come to know You through him." Since they had decided to keep this a secret between them and God, I didn't know about their prayer for many years.

I clearly remember that, as I entered my teen years, I was concerned about my future. I told my mother, "My friends already know what they're going to do when they grow up. I don't have a clue."

She didn't want to pressure me with her heart's desire, so she just said: "You don't know what you will do, Luis, but God does. He will show it to you at the right time."

Boyhood heroes

My mother read missionary stories to my sisters and me, over and over, before we went to sleep many a cold winter's night. My favorite was the true story of Mildred Cable and Francesca French, who carried the Gospel through Asia (particularly the Gobi desert) in spite of tremendous persecution and physical abuse. That story would come back to me later and convict me of my need to share Christ.

My mother recently went to be with the Lord, at age eighty-three. To talk about her is to talk about someone who was a tremendous blessing in my life. And to talk about my father evokes the same emotions in me.

My dad was consistent, the same person at home as he was at church. He rose early on cold winter mornings to start a wood fire in the stove. I should have been sleeping, but often I sneaked out of bed just to watch him putter around the house.

If I watched long enough, I might see him go into his office—a little study he built on one side of the house—and kneel alone. In those days we didn't have central heating, so he would wrap himself in a blanket or poncho. Then he would read the Bible and pray before going out to work. Though I was not even seven years old yet, I would steal back to my bed, feeling warm and grateful that I had a good dad.

One day he told me that he read a chapter from Proverbs every day, since it has thirty-one chapters and there are thirty-one days in most months. His example stuck with me, and I still try to practice it. I have told so many friends and associates that story that many, many people now do the same. In spite of all the other Bible studying and reading I do, I try to start the day with my chapter from Proverbs. And many a time I read it on my knees.

I practically idolized my father. I loved to say my name was "Luis Palau, Jr." He was my ideal of a man, even though he was quiet and humble for a person of such stature in the church and community. I have a choleric personality, on the other hand, and have learned I must constantly put my quick temper under the control of Christ.

What bothers me is my temper rages over the little things in life, not the big issues. If I were the victim of another driver's carelessness and he caused an accident, I could be cool as a cucumber. But let me knock over a glass and suddenly I fly off the handle. I am not proud of this tendency, but I would be a hypocrite to say it hasn't been a problem.

When I was a child, my temper flared up every time something was wrong or I didn't get my own way. I was persistent to a fault, moaning and groaning and pestering my mother for days, begging her to give in on some issue or another. In retrospect, I'm sure she was too nice to me. She should have dealt with me strongly!

As a child I was burdened with a tremendous sense of guilt because I couldn't control my tongue. I could shout and say the meanest things. If I felt I had been unfairly treated in a soccer game, I would use some of the worst language on the field.

Even though I had not yet actually trusted Jesus Christ as my Savior, I was proud that my dad and mom were committed Christians. When we rode on benches in the back of one of my dad's trucks and folded evangelistic Gospel tracts to pass out in a neighboring town, I reacted to the taunts and insults with resolve. I saw the religious parades, common on the many holidays in Latin America, and I determined that one day biblical Christians would do the same things, emphasizing salvation through Jesus Christ.

When a child is thrust into a position in which he must stand firm for the Lord in the face of opposition, I believe he is strengthened by it. It's much more valuable to our spiritual lives when we have to stand up for our beliefs in a non-Christian environment.

So I had an evangelistic fervor—perhaps not for the right reason—even before I actually became a committed Christian.

Until my oldest sister, Matilde, joined me a couple of years after I started, I was the only child of evangelical Christian parents in the local government public school. I was called names occasionally, even by the teachers, who made me kneel in the corner on corn kernels if I misbehaved.

British schooling

By the time I was seven, my father decided it was time to send me to Quilmes Preparatory School, a private British boarding school near the capital. He wanted the best possible education for me and dreamed of one day sending me to study at Cambridge University in England. He also knew it would be to my advantage to become completely bilingual, equally fluent in English and Spanish.

Although I missed my parents and family a great deal, I enjoyed my classes, sports, and other activities at the boarding school and was able to go home one weekend each month. My maternal grandparents lived only a couple of streets away from the school, but I was not allowed to visit or even call them. When you're at school, you're at school. The British were rather disciplined about such things. They had rules and regulations and schedules for everything. I needed that! And I live it out still today.

It didn't take me long to improve my English, though learning it from Britishers gave me a bit of a strange combined accent—strange, at least, to Americans—when I first arrived in the States years later.

Quilmes was good preparation for St. Alban's College, where I was scheduled to go when I was ten years old. Shortly after my tenth birthday, I took all my final exams at Quilmes and began to prepare for the trip home. Instead of my parents coming to pick me up, however, I received a call from my grandmother. She was not supposed to call me at school, so I knew something was wrong.

"Luis," she said, ignoring any amenities, "your dad is very sick. We really have to pray for him." Although she gave me no details, I had a terrible feeling he was dead or dying. The next morning, December 17, 1944, Grandma came to put me on a train bound for home.

"It's serious," she said. "Your mom wants you to come and see your dad."

The three-hour trip seemed interminable. I couldn't stand it. I wished I could have engineered the train myself and sped things up. I loved my dad more than ever. Although we had been apart more than half the time the past three years, we had talked at length and made many plans.

But now I couldn't shake this ominous feeling. I was sure my father was already gone.

2

I sat in silence on the train, staring ahead, yet seeing nothing. There was no way I could ignore the dread, the certainty that I would arrive too late to say goodbye to my father.

I didn't even know what was wrong with my dad. I wouldn't learn until later that he had suffered for just ten days. Bronchial pneumonia had been diagnosed and nothing could be done. December 1944 was not a good time to need penicillin. It was all locked up in Europe and the Pacific, helping mop up the end of World War II.

When the train finally reached Ingeniero-Maschwitz, I was out of my seat and pressing up against the door. I bounded down the steps and ran toward home. The blast-furnace temperature didn't deter me. It was the hottest day of the year, but to me it seemed wrong to see people lounging around, sipping soft drinks, and fanning themselves. Something was terribly wrong at my house, yet people in town were lazing around.

Any shred of hope I might have harbored in the back of my mind during the long train ride was quickly dispelled when I came within earshot of my house and heard the traditional wailing. Some of my non-Christian aunts and uncles were moaning and crying and asking, "Why does God allow this? So many little children left without a father. Oh, what will Matilde do?"

Relatives tried to intercept me as I ran through the gate and up to the house; I brushed past them and was in the door before my mother even knew I was there. And there was my father: yellow, bloated, still secreting fluid, blood drying, lips cracked. His body had dehydrated.

I ran to him, ignoring my sisters Matilde, Martha, Ketty, and Margarita, and all my other relatives. My father was in bed, as if asleep. He had died just a few hours earlier.

Father's death

I tried to steel myself in the midst of all the crying and sobbing, but I began to shake. I couldn't believe this! I would never talk with my father again. He looked terrible, but I wanted him to be all right. I hugged him and kissed him, but he was gone.

My mother—stunned but not crying—stepped behind me and put her hands on my shoulders. "Luisito, Luisito," she said softly, pulling me away. "I must talk to you and tell you how it was."

She took me outside, and I tried to stifle my sobs while listening to her account. "When the doctors realized they weren't able to do anything else for him, we decided to call you so you could hurry home. It was obvious he was dying, and as we gathered around his bed, praying and trying to comfort him, he seemed to fall asleep. He was struggling to breathe, but suddenly he sat up and began to sing."

I looked up at my mother, hardly believing what she was telling me.

"Papito began to sing," she said, "'Bright crowns up there, bright crowns for you and me. Then the palm of victory, the palm of victory.' He sang it three times, all the while clapping in time as you children did when you sang it in Sunday school.

"Then, when Papito could no longer hold up his head, he fell back on the pillow and said, 'I'm going to be with Jesus, which is far better.'" A short time later, he went to be with the Lord.

It was painful for me to mull over my mother's story of how my father had died, but I couldn't push it out of my mind. That he was sure of heaven was the only minutely positive element in the whole ordeal. That picture is still so vivid to me that I sometimes almost feel as if I had been there when he was singing. It was such a contrast to the typical Latin American scene, where the dying person cries out in fear of going to hell.

Still, my grief devastated me, and I was angry at everything and everyone. It wasn't fair. Why couldn't my father die in old age like everyone else?

It hurt to walk by my father's little study. I didn't want to see anything that reminded me of him. There was no comforting me. My world, my future, had come to an end. Even my father's dog howled as dogs tend to do when they sense their master is gone.

Because there was no embalming, the dead person had to be buried quickly, usually within twenty-four hours. Once the doctor or care-taker had cleaned the body and laid it in a casket, family and friends gathered around the bereaved to support and comfort them.

That was a horrible night. I didn't want to be there, and I didn't want to leave. I was a jumble of ten-year-old emotions. People sat around drinking coffee and talking in whispers. Since there would be very little time before the burial, relatives in distant towns were contacted and began arriving at different times all night.

Many found it difficult to stay awake with my mother, so there were people sleeping in beds, chairs, and on the floor all over the house. I tried to be a man and stay awake all night, but eventually the trip and the trauma got to me, and I fell into a fitful sleep.

Death became, to me, the ultimate reality. Everything else can be rationalized and wondered about and discussed, but death is there, staring you in the face. It's real. It happens. He was there, and now he's gone, and that's it.

Making sure of heaven

Without a doubt, the death of my father has had more impact on my ministry than anything else in my entire life, besides my own conversion to Jesus Christ. My wish and desire is that people get right with God, settle the big question, and die happy, knowing they will be with Jesus, "which is better by far" (Philippians 1:23).

For days on end that summer, my mother was mercilessly peppered with my questions about heaven, the second coming of Jesus Christ, and the resurrection. It was good she had been a Christian for more than eight years and was a student of the Scriptures. She had the answers I needed to hear again and again.

She had her own grief and loss to deal with, and perhaps this was one way she did it. By reminding me and assuring me and my sisters of the truths of Scripture all day, every day, she was probably simultaneously applying therapy to her own soul.

She drilled the words of the Lord Jesus into us:

Do not let your hearts be troubled. Trust in God; trust also in me. In my Father's house are many rooms; if it were not so, I would have told you. I am going there to prepare a place for you. And if I go and prepare a place for you, I will come back and take you to be with me that you also may be where I am (John 14:1-3).

We memorized that portion, along with the apostle Paul's words:

Brothers, we do not want you to be ignorant about those who fall asleep, or to grieve like the rest of men, who have no hope. We believe that Jesus died and rose again and so we believe that God will bring with Jesus those who have fallen asleep in him (1 Thessalonians 4:13-14).

The things of eternity and heaven became so settled in my mind during those few months before going off to a new school that I have never been ashamed to preach on heaven. Some people have become a little skittish about it in recent years, claiming we really don't know much about heaven, whether it's literal or symbolic.

I don't believe we should go around mocking the streets of gold. Even if it *is* symbolic, why mock symbols? Scripture says the streets are gold, so let the streets be gold. When we get there, we'll find out exactly what God meant. Anyone with any imagination should realize that heaven will be astonishing, superb, glorious. If God depicted it as decorated with the most precious metals and jewels on earth, let that be so. Enlightened imagination is called for and God-given.

I just can't imagine facing eternity or even losing a loved one without having the absolute assurance of heaven and all its ramifications. Through the years I have thought how lucky my father was to have arrived there so far ahead of the rest of us. And now my mother has gone to be with him. They're in perfect bliss. They're happy. They're having a great time. They're in the presence of the Lord, forever. If I didn't believe that with all my heart, I'd give it all up.

Going to heaven someday is as real to me as if I said I was going to fly to Chicago or Miami or Los Angeles or New York and meet you for lunch. When I get off the plane, I fully expect to see you there, waiting for me. That's the way it will be with seeing Jesus and my loved ones when I die.

Malcolm Muggeridge says, in A *20th-Century Testimony*:

Death is a beginning, not an end. The darkness falls, and in the sky is a distant glow, the lights of St. Augustine's City of God. Looking towards them, I say over to myself John Donne's splendid words: *Death thou shalt die.* In the graveyard, the dust settles; in the City of God, eternity begins.

It's hard to understand why more people don't come to Christ just because of heaven. It's the best bargain there is. You give up yourself, let Jesus take over, receive forgiveness of sin, and are assured of eternal life with Him. Frankly, I cannot fathom the logic of people who know all God is offering and still say they don't want to be saved.

People who know me best say I preach about heaven with more power—not with human words, of course, but with a God-given sense of reality and a passion for souls—than when I preach about anything else. I can feel my heart almost bursting from my body as I attempt to draw more people to Jesus Christ.

Larry's story

When I go to a city for an evangelistic crusade, I often do a live call-in television counseling program called *NightTalk with Luis Palau*. You never know what to expect from city to city. Crank calls? Viewers upset that a favorite program has been pre-empted? Will anyone call?

Suddenly, we're on the air. "This is a live program here on Fox 35," I told viewers in San Antonio. "We're not here to kill time or debate religion. We're here to talk with you live, over the phone, about problems or concerns you might have right now."

Larry, a thirty-two-year-old man dying of AIDS, was up late for *Arsenio Hall* on Channel 35. Afterward, he watched *NightTalk* for a few minutes, then called to talk with me. "I'm going through a living hell," he said, then broke into tears while on the air.

As tens of thousands of viewers watched, I had the privilege of counseling Larry and leading him to faith in Jesus Christ. He received forgiveness for his sins, joined God's forever family, and received eternal life.

Off the air, we got Larry's address and phone number, then made sure he began receiving immediate, compassionate follow-up care from trained counselors from a local church. Before his tragic death, how great it was to hear Larry express his hope of heaven!

The next night, and many times since then the past couple of years, I've used Larry's story to lead still others to Christ. In fact, I probably use more stories when I preach about heaven then I do at any other time. Some say it's wrong to appeal to people's emotions. You can't preach the Gospel devoid of solid intellectual and doctrinal truth, of course. But come now. We have emotions, don't we? God gave them to us for a purpose. If the story of counseling an AIDS victim or the story of my father's death helps propel someone to come to Christ, then I say, so be it. Praise the Lord. Let them come.

Three months after my father's death, summer drew to a close and the time came for me to go to St. Alban's College, connected with the Cambridge University Overseas Program. What once had been a dream I now viewed with indifference. But my mother said that Dad had already decided to send me there, and she wanted to follow through with his wishes.

Meanwhile, my mother hired someone to manage the family business, because she never had been involved in it and didn't know what else to do. That decision eventually would prove financially disastrous, but none of us knew it then. We had always had all the money we needed, and I didn't have an inkling that it would ever end.

St. Alban's was a tough, all-boys, Anglican school. The Argentine government required that at least four hours a day, five days a week, be taught in Spanish. Because St. Alban's was a British school, they met the requirement and then taught the rest of the school day in English.

But we did not do the same lessons in English in the afternoon that we had learned in the morning in Spanish. We moved ahead in our courses. We became totally bilingual, and we got two years of schooling every year. By the time you were finished, you had the equivalent of four years of high school and several more years of college and, like our British counterparts, were qualified for graduate work at Cambridge University.

St. Alban's was an expensive, exclusive private school. (I don't mean that to sound snobbish, but that's what it was.) Fortunately, my father provided for me and saw the value in my attending such a place. I became involved in all of the activities, particularly athletics.

About half of the students were British, the sons of railway, banking, shipping, or lumber executives. Because of the cost, the other students were from at least middle-class families. All of us— from the youngest to the oldest—wore British private-school uniforms. We all got up at the same time, made our beds, cleaned our areas, and brushed and combed our hair just so. We stood in line, marched, and obeyed our "masters." And we were disciplined when we didn't.

We both hated and loved it. We were proud of our discipline, of our school, and that we knew what was proper. We had been trained to be responsible, and for the most part we did what we were told.

Perhaps not everyone belongs in such a boarding school, but for me it was basically good and healthy; and for the most part, I liked it. I hesitate to think what I might have become had I not lived under that discipline and been expected to learn self-control.

Some of the older and more rebellious boys would run off without permission and buy a beer, which they drank way up in the woods at the back of the school property. If they were reported, they would more likely lie than admit it, putting off the cricket-bat punishment for as long as they could.

There was nothing like having to bend over, touch your toes, and wait for the swing and sting of that massive, flat bat. I ought to know, as you will see.

Though my grades were always pretty good, for a long time I had a poor attitude. My feeling was, "I'll study when I want to and not just because the professor says I have to."

In spite of that, those were happy days for me. We had our fun with the teachers and with one another. Pranks, jokes, traps—anything was fair game.

Love of sports

The British were so well-organized that the games and sports were really fun, even though they looked down their noses at Latin America's number one sport, soccer. Soccer was for "naps"—street people, the uneducated—and prohibited on campus in favor of cricket, rugby, and the sort.

But then as now, school rules stand little chance against a boy's heart. With other daring classmates behind a grove of trees on the edge of the school grounds, I'd nurture my dream of winning the World Cup with a spectacular last-second goal.

I suppose I enjoyed sports because it kept me from growing up too fast. With my father gone, I felt bombarded from every side. My aunts and uncles started saying I was the man of the family and would be expected to take over the family business someday and care for my mother and sisters. I was eleven years old, and already I had to try to decide if I thought I could handle such heavy responsibilities. Even thinking of my father's business brought back painful memories of his death. How could I run a business that carried such memories?

I eventually began to realize the family business was no longer what it had been when my father was alive. Over the summer, my mother began to worry about whether she could afford to send me back to St.

Alban's. That nearly made me panic. St. Alban's was the world I really knew and loved. And it kept me from having to think about my awesome responsibilities too soon.

My mother wasn't even sure she could afford to send me to a camp that one of my teachers, Charles Cohen, wanted me to go to during summer vacation. But she certainly wanted me to go. Mr. Cohen was one of the few evangelicals in our Anglican school, and when he took boys on camping trips, several usually came back as new Christians.

My mother knew I had not made a definite commitment to Christ yet, and she encouraged me to go to camp. I didn't want to go, and I was determined to use our quickly deteriorating financial situation as my alibi.

3

A t St. Alban's, Mr. Cohen talked to me about going to his two-week camp in the mountains with several dozen other boys. It sounded like fun, but I didn't want to go. I would have to be away from my family when I was supposed to be home on vacation, and I knew camp would be overly evangelistic. Someone would definitely put the pressure on me to receive Jesus Christ, I was sure.

Oh, if someone asked, I could stand up and quote many Bible verses. I could sing a lot of songs. I could even say a prayer if you put me on the spot. But in my heart, I knew I wasn't a real Christian.

When I put Mr. Cohen off, he smiled and let me paint myself into a corner. As soon as I pretended I wanted to go—"but can't because of my family's tight financial situation"—he offered to pay my way. It was off to camp for me, despite my wishes. Even several of my buddies refused to go with me.

By the end of the school year in 1946 (early in December, just before summer in South America), I had turned twelve and headed home for several weeks before camp began in February. It was annoying to have been caught and forced to go—which was not the "in" thing to do—but by the time February rolled around, I was anxious to head for the mountains.

My mother told me straight out she was glad I was going, because she wasn't sure I was a real, born-again Christian. I responded, "Mom, come on," trying to pretend I was. But she knew better.

Learning about sex

If I wasn't exactly straightforward with my mother when it came to spiritual matters, she definitely wasn't open about talking to me about girls, sexuality, birth, and so on. I had heard a lot of talk at school from the older students, which made me as curious as any twelve-year-old boy, and maybe a bit more so. I just had to know what it was all about, and I hounded my mother for details.

She kept telling me that she'd discuss it with me when I was thirteen, probably hoping that someone else would save her the trouble by then. It was too much to ask a widowed mother in those days, but I kept pestering her and pestering her. She would not give in. I wish she had.

I have always resented the fact that not once—even during all of my teen years—did a Christian man take me aside and try to fill my father's shoes and openly talk to me about sex—or anything else, for that matter.

I think it's an indictment on the Church that we let boys and girls learn about sex from someone outside the church or family. Many of them fail and fall into sin, partially because of their ignorance, and we are quick to condemn them (and abandon them), assuming they should have known something that we failed to teach them.

Anyway, that summer my sexual advisor was a twenty-year-old worker who drove the truck in the family business. I was helping him deliver a load of cement bags and was really enjoying jumping in and out of the cab and feeling like a man. Then one day he pulled over to the side of the road and pulled out a magazine from his pocket. At first I couldn't tell what it was.

"Luisito," he said, "since you are becoming a young man now"—I sat up a bit straighter, appreciating the stroke to my ego—"and you have no father, you need someone to talk to you about the facts of life."

My heart began to pound. I was excited to think I might get some straight answers from someone who really knew the score. "I want to make a man of you," he said. But instead of telling me anything, he simply opened his magazine and turned the pages while I stared in disbelief. I was shocked and disgusted, but of course I couldn't take my eyes off the page.

I had never seen anything that revealing. I knew it was all wrong; it was dirty; it wasn't pure; yet I was curious. I couldn't sort out my emotions. It was appalling, yet appealing at the same time. I wanted to see it, yet I hated it.

There were fifty or sixty pictures in his magazine. The fact that he would show me something like that shocked me. I couldn't even speak. If he had asked me the next day if I wanted to see the magazine again, I would have run the other way.

I could not push those images out of my mind. I felt horrible, degraded, sinful. My mother would have died, if she'd known what happened. I felt guilty all the time, and especially in the presence of my mother or anyone from the local church. I was certain people could read guilt all over my face.

Impure thoughts invaded my mind. Of course, I had all the usual daydreams about wanting to love someone and marry her, and as my sexual awareness increased, I even dreamed of romantic love. But now everything had been spoiled. I had been curious before. Now I was repulsed. And why had I not been able to look away? I feared the judgment of God.

I was haunted by the idea that others might be thinking the same things about my sisters and my mother that I was thinking about the women in their families. My church emphasized holiness and purity, and my mother's holy life made me revere the opposite sex. Yet the impulses within me had now been twisted by what I had seen.

Not knowing that I was hardly unique among boys my age who'd had their first shocking encounter with pornography, I could not reconcile it in my mind. It was wrong, and yet it held fascination. I was in such a state that I was actually glad I was going to camp!

Summer camp

I had never been to camp before, so trekking off into a hilly, mountainous area called Azul in southern Argentina carried its own special sense of excitement. I tried to forget about the sins of my mind, because I got a dreadful feeling in the pit of my stomach when I thought of it.

At the Christian camp run by Mr. Cohen, I recognized most of the boys from St. Alban's. We used Argentine army tents and brought our own foldable cots, which we set up ourselves. It was almost like the Scouts.

We set up our tents, dug trenches around them, policed the area, and generally were taught how to "rough it." There were probably fifty or sixty boys in all, supervised by Mr. Cohen and several counselors from different missionary organizations.

The counselors were all Britishers or Americans concerned for the spiritual welfare of their campers. We had Bible lessons, memorization, and singing every day, along with the usual fun and games.

I missed the contact with the outside world. There were no radios, no newspapers, no nothing. We couldn't even hear the soccer scores. We were totally cut off. We were saturated with the Word of God and with happy, snappy Gospel songs, many of which have stuck with me to this day.

One morning an American Bible teacher spoke on purity in that ambiguous, roundabout way many people have of dealing with the subject of sex. His talk didn't give me the detailed instruction I needed, but it was very helpful for one reason. It was obvious this man knew what he was talking about, and even as refined as he was about discussing the subject, his view of its sanctity and sacredness came through. More than anything, I was impressed that he himself was a pure man in an impure world.

I assumed most people were as coarse as they boasted they were, and I still felt bad about my own confused thoughts on the subject. But this Bible teacher impressed me and gave me hope that there were indeed pure Christian men—men I could model myself after. Though I was attracted by the images in my mind, somehow I knew what was right. And this godly teacher affirmed that.

It was strange to see the stiff, curt, formal, aloof Mr. Cohen— whom I had know from St. Alban's as someone above it all—in khaki shorts and a totally different setting. He even acted a little differently, almost as if he had a sense of humor. The little jokes he cracked were incongruous with his station in life and his personality, and that made them even funnier. It was almost as if he were on our level. I was beginning to like camp, but I knew that soon someone was going to confront me about my faith.

Appointment in the night

It happened every evening. Each counselor had about ten boys in his tent, and each night one boy was taken for a walk and given the opportunity to say yes or no to Christ's claims upon his life. After the second night everyone knew his turn was coming, because the first two kids were telling everyone what had happened.

- If you really didn't want to receive Christ, they wouldn't force you, of course. This was a making-sure exercise. Many of these kids had already received Christ, and the counselors were helping to solidify their decision and give them biblical assurance. Then there were the boys like me, who had grown up in solid, evangelistic churches and knew the whole story, yet had never accepted it for themselves.

Even the unchurched boys knew the plan of salvation by the end of the two weeks, and many of them made Christian commitments during those little after-dark walks with their counselors. Some have wondered why I'm so enthusiastic about Christian camping. Now you know. It moves me to think how concerned those counselors were and how effective that system was, in spite of its rigid programming. No one was badgered or forced, but no one missed his opportunity to receive Christ, either.

Finally my appointment with destiny arrived. Every other boy in my tent had talked with our counselor, Frank Chandler. When he came into the tent that last night of camp, I knew why!

I wanted to run and hide, I was so embarrassed I had not received Christ yet; still, I couldn't lie and say that I had.

Even though I felt guilty for my sins and knew I needed to make a Christian commitment, I didn't want to face the issue with anyone. I pretended I was asleep, thinking Frank would go away. It didn't work. He shook me, but I continued to act sound asleep. He knew I was faking, so he picked up the cot and dumped me onto the ground. Obviously, I couldn't pretend I was sleeping after that!

"Come on, Luis," my counselor said, "get up." I didn't know it, but this was going to be the best night of camp.

Frank and I went outside and sat down on a fallen tree. It was cold and a light rain was beginning to fall. A thunderstorm was coming our way. Frank knew he had to hurry. He pulled out his flashlight and opened his New Testament. "Luis," he asked, "are you a born-again Christian or not?"

I said, "I don't think so."

"Well, it's not a matter of whether you think so or not. Are you or aren't you?"

"No, I'm not."

4

"If you died tonight," Frank asked me, "would you go to heaven or hell?"

I sat quietly for a moment, a bit taken aback, and then said, "I'm going to hell."

"Is that where you want to go?"

"No," I replied.

"Then why are you going there?"

I shrugged my shoulders. "I don't know."

Frank then turned in his Bible to the apostle Paul's letter to the Romans and read: "If you confess with your lips, [Luis], that Jesus is Lord and believe in your heart, [Luis], that God raised him from the dead, you, [Luis], will be saved. For man believes with his heart and so is justified, and he confesses with his lips and so is saved" (Romans 10:9-10 RSV).

Frank looked back at me. "Luis, do you believe in your heart that God raised Jesus from the dead?"

"Yes, I do," I said.

"Then what do you have to do next to be saved?"

I hesitated as it began to rain even harder. Frank had me read Romans 10:9 once more—"If you confess with your lips that Jesus is Lord...you will be saved."

"Luis, are you ready to confess Him as your Lord right now?"

"Yes."

"All right, let's pray." Frank put his arm around me and led me in a prayer. I opened my heart to Christ right there, out in the rain sitting on a log, in a hurry, but I made my decision. I prayed, "Lord Jesus, I believe You were raised from the dead. I confess You with my lips. Give me eternal life. I want to be Yours. Save me from hell. Amen."

Most important decision

When we finished praying, I was crying. I gave Frank a big hug and we ran back into the tent. I crawled under my blanket with my flashlight and wrote in my Bible "February 12, 1947" and "I received Jesus Christ."

I was only twelve years old at the time, but I knew I was born again. I was saved. I was a member of the family of God. I had eternal life because Jesus Christ said, "I give them eternal life, and they shall never perish; no one can snatch them out of my hand" (John 10:28).

I could hardly sleep, I was so excited about committing my life to Christ. After all, it is the most important decision anyone can ever make. Compared to eternal life, all other decisions aren't that important when you think about it.

C. S. Lewis, the famous English author and Oxford professor, said it well, "No one is ready to live life on earth until he is ready for life in heaven."

I think back on the night of my conversion often, especially when I hear people criticize speed and technique in evangelism. We worry about hurrying a person in his decision; but, I tell you, when the person is ready, just get to the point and help him or her settle the issue. When you sense the Holy Spirit at work, time and technique can be irrelevant.

My mother was ecstatic, of course, which was opposite the reaction I received from my friend George James and others at school. I wasn't obnoxious about it; I just was so thrilled about my commitment that I wanted them to know. I even carried my Bible with me a lot.

I was more active in the Crusaders youth group, and the Anglican church services we were required to attend weekly took on a whole new meaning for me. I was even christened and confirmed. I sang in the choir, until my terrible voice got me drubbed out, and I began to study my Bible every day. I corresponded often with Frank Chandler and still have many of his letters to this day. And I became a much better student, especially in Mr. Cohen's Acts of the Apostles class.

The biblical classes at St. Alban's grew more significant to me, and I really studied hard and learned. I could visualize the cities and movement of the early church in Acts, it was so clearly taught. Years later, when I studied the same course at the seminary level in the United States, I found I already knew most of it from that semester as a twelve-year-old, when I was immersed in my first love of Christ. There's not a more open and teachable mind than that of a child still excited over his conversion.

I felt closer to Mr. Cohen and really pitched in to help at Crusaders youth group meetings held in his home on Sunday afternoons. I sang out, listened hard, and studied all my Bible lessons. It was a beautiful experience, even though it alienated me from some of my friends who were still into dirty stories and other shenanigans.

Missionary heroes

That year our Crusader club was visited by two old missionary ladies from China, Mildred Cable and Francesca French. They had tremendous stories to tell of their travels through the Gobi Desert in the interior of China, and of being dragged through the streets of pagan cities because they insisted upon sharing Christ with the Chinese.

In spite of all the physical abuse and punishment and persecution, Mildred and Francesca stayed on for years in China, spreading the Gospel of Jesus Christ. Their witness hit me at just the right time in my life to make the best impression on me. I thought I had become an outspoken Christian, but what was I doing, compared to these women? Then I remembered that they were the very two missionaries my mother had read about to me and my sisters when we were little.

I began to look for more missionary books. I was inspired to read about how men and women gave up the luxuries of life to minister under adverse conditions, just because they loved the Lord and wanted to serve Him. I prayed that I, too, would love the Lord like that.

I didn't know whether I was going to be a missionary, but I knew I wanted to do something for God. I was getting the broadest possible background for it. I was attending one of the "highest" worship services imaginable every week in the Anglican church. And I had grown up in what might be termed the humblest, most nonconformist church, the Christian Brethren.

I feel I'm in a unique position to love and relate to people from a broad variety of backgrounds because of the diversity of my childhood religious training. From one of the most hierarchical churches in the world one Sunday to the least organized the next Sunday, I was an excited, eager listener and learner.

One thing I gained from the Anglican church was an appreciation for the beautiful language possible in prayer. I had been dissatisfied with my prayer life; my prayers seemed to just slip into repetitious blessings of Mom, sisters, and relatives. The Anglican prayers can be repetitious, too, but what a blessing they can be if you let yourself think about their beautiful and deep content. One of my favorites— and one I use occasionally in my private devotions even now—is:

We have left undone those things
which we ought to have done;
And we have done those things
which we ought not to have done;
And there is no health in us.

The loss of that first excitement and love for the Gospel is something no one has ever been able to explain adequately. It happens to so many, and when I lost it, it was as if someone had pulled my plug and the lights had gone out. Perhaps I let a cynical attitude get in the way. Perhaps I ignored my mother's counsel to stay away from worldly influences, like listening to soccer matches on Sunday and going to movies, and perhaps I was succumbing to the pressures of my fellow students.

Cooling off spiritually

All I know is that one day, coming home from Crusaders, I carelessly left my Bible on a streetcar and was unable to get it back. With that loss went my daily Bible reading, my attendance at Crusaders, my excitement over Bible classes, and almost everything else that went along with my commitment to Christ. I still loved and believed and respected the Gospel, but I did not let it interfere with my life.

I did not totally understand this quick turn-off myself, but part of it may have had to do with the punishment I received one day at the hands of Mr. Cohen. The fearful role of disciplinarian was rotated among the professors. That day, Mr. Cohen was the teacher in charge of campus order. I was in an art class and doing none too well.

I was showing off to some of my friends when Mr. Thompson, the new art teacher, walked over, took a puff from his distinguished looking pipe, and made a rather sarcastic remark about my horrible painting of a tree. He was right, of course; it was horrible. But as he walked away, I responded with some foul word in Spanish, which Mr. Thompson, recently come from England, was not supposed to understand. The rest of the class understood me just fine and laughed.

"What did you say, Palau?" he asked.

"Oh, nothing, Mr. Thompson, sir. Nothing, really."

"No, what was it, Palau?"

"It was really nothing important, sir."

"I'd really like to hear it again, Palau. Would you mind repeating it?"

"Oh, I don't think it's worth repeating. I . . . ."

"All right," Mr. Thompson snapped. "Go see the master on duty."

The class fell silent, and my jaw dropped. That was the ultimate punishment. No one else tells the master on duty why you are there. You must tell him yourself and take whatever punishment he deems necessary. I almost died inside when I saw Mr. Cohen was on duty.

"Come in, Palau," he said. "Why are you here?"

"Mr. Thompson sent me."

"Is that so? Why?"

Mr. Cohen was being terribly cold, especially for someone I knew and with whom I had spent a lot of time. He was even a fellow Christian, but here he was, aloof and frigid again.

"Well, I said a bad word," I confessed.

"Repeat it," he said.

"Oh, I had better not," I said.

"Repeat it," he insisted.

There was no way out of it. One little word in art class. And now all this. I told Mr. Cohen what I had said. He didn't move at first. He just sat there staring at me, obviously disappointed, but mostly disgusted with me. When he finally spoke, it sounded like the voice of God. He reached for the cricket bat—he was a pretty fair player, and he knew how to swing it.

"You know, Palau, I'm going to give you six of the best." It was the maximum amount of swats for any punishment.

I froze.

5

"Bend and touch your toes, please."

As I slowly bent over, Mr. Cohen said, "Before I punish you, I want to tell you this, Palau. You are the greatest hypocrite I have ever seen in my life."

I winced. That sounded pretty strong.

"You think you get away with your arrogant, cynical, above-it-all, know-it-all attitude, but I have watched you. You come to Bible class, all right, but you are a hypocrite."

That hurt almost as much as the six shots I took to my seat. The physical punishment stung for days, and I mean literally *days*. It was hard to sit down, and I slept on my stomach for a week. I cried and cried, as tough as I wanted to be about it. What Mr. Cohen said and what he did were both medicine for me, but it took years before I realized it.

For months I hated the man. I wouldn't look at him, let alone say hello or smile at him. I quit going to Crusaders, and I quit paying attention in his Bible classes. I went through the motions of going to church because we had to, but I acted totally indifferent to the services. And I was.

Something between God and me had been severed. Not my salvation, of course, but something sweet in the relationship. I started to stretch the limits that had been placed on me by my school, my mother, and the church. At that time I believed it was sinful to go to school dances or read magazines about car racing and sports on Sunday, but I did it anyway. I joined my old friends, began talking rough again, and generally developed a bad attitude toward life.

It doesn't sound like much now, but back then it was the height of shaking my fist in the face of all I had been taught. I had been an excited, eager, happy Christian for almost a year. And now I was flat.

Poor witness

I felt worldly and sinful and guilty, but somehow I couldn't come out of it. Very simply, I did not live for God during the rest of my school years at St. Alban's and my summers at home. I knew deep down inside that I belonged to Christ, but the pressure not to be considered a fool was too much for me.

I stood by and let the two or three other born-again Christians at St. Alban's carry the ball for the Gospel. Henry Martin and David Leake were two of the other committed Christians, and I always felt sorry that I was hardly in their league as a witness.

Leake, now a bishop in the Anglican church, didn't flaunt his faith. He was simply faithful and steady. He never talked piously. He was just himself, and he was admired and respected.

Henry Martin, who still lives in the town where I grew up, was aggressively outspoken for Christ. He made sure others knew he wouldn't dance or enjoy worldly pleasures on Sunday or engage in the occasional beer-drinking escapades. He never hassled the masters, either, even when everyone else did.

At one point, we grew so tired of having the same menu week after week that we staged a mild rebellion. Everyone took just a few grains of rice and put them on his plate, leaving the huge serving bowls full at each table. When the masters came around and demanded to know why no one was eating rice, everyone pointed at his plate and said, "I had some! See?" Everyone, that is, except Henry Martin. He would not be part of any disrespectful actions, so he ate a generous portion of rice. The others threatened to beat the stuffing out of him later, but he told them straight out he didn't think it was right and he couldn't go along with them in good conscience because he was a Christian.

Later they made good on their threat. As I stood and watched, several of the bigger boys beat him bloody. I felt so bad for so long about watching that happen to someone who stood up for the Lord that, twenty years later, I contacted Henry and apologized. He forgave me but had totally forgotten the incident long ago.

Over the years I've tried to determine just what went wrong with my spiritual temperature during those last years of school. I certainly had no idea about how to live a victorious life. I had been well taught, but I was into a spirituality based on performance. I had no goals and little idea of my own resources. I just knew what I had to do or not do to be a fine Christian.

It was a nice, mild form of legalism. Praying, reading the Bible, studying, and going to church can wear thin fast, if that's all there is to a person's faith. I don't recall picking up any instruction on how to enjoy the indwelling Lord Jesus Christ, how to walk with Him and be happy in Him. How to really praise and worship God for who He is slipped past me, and I found myself bored with simply going on and on in the same old routine.

Although I take full responsibility myself, several things contributed to my straying into the world. The first was that my father had not left a will, and the individual who took over the management of our family business defrauded us and left us destitute. I was not equipped to forgive him, and the rage I felt as a teenager is hard to describe. When I understood more how that man had jeopardized the very survival of my widowed mother and her children, I felt like I could have destroyed him.

Second, there was the lure of the world and non-Christian friends. They seemed to have so much more fun. I was drawn into a life of parties and soccer games and listening to the radio—hardly bad things in themselves, but indicative of my loss of interest in spiritual things.

Because of the business failure, my mother did everything she could to see that I continued in school. Since I was part British, a British charity gave me a partial subsidy on my tuition. But I was forced to live with my grandparents in Quilmes and commute to school to save money. It was somewhat humiliating, and it also put me in a position to be less disciplined about whom I spent my time with.

Fortunately, even my non-Christian friends from my new neighborhood were pretty straight, or I could have gotten into big trouble. We wasted time by sitting around and talking for hours, but what really made me feel guilty was spending my Sundays doing something other than Christian work.

My dream was to become a race-car driver, a soccer player, or a big businessman. Even though the family was nearly bankrupt and the business was virtually finished, I told my friends it was thriving and just waiting for me to come back and run it.

I was going to be rich and powerful, I boasted, a self-made businessman. Only I was lying. And I knew it full well. During those really low years when I was in my mid-teens and living with my grandparents, doing my own thing, I actually blamed God for most of our troubles. I had come full circle from my first love of Him to where I thought He had let us down.

Cambridge dreams dashed

Finally things got so financially desperate that my mother came to tell me I could not continue much longer. I could complete what would be the equivalent of a junior college degree in the United States, but I would not be able to take the last year and qualify for the graduate program at Cambridge.

Completing the Cambridge program was a dream I had nurtured for years. Even though I was a rebellious student, my grades had been good, and I looked forward to continuing my education in England. Short of that, I at least wanted to further my education in the capital city, but that was out of the question. I would have to go to work to help support my family, and they were going to have to move several hundred miles north to Cordoba, now that there was nothing left of the business.

I felt I had been the victim of a cruel joke. Eight long, double years of schooling in the British boarding schools would leave me with an intermediate degree, no money, and no future, as far as I could tell. I still feared God, but I questioned Him daily and was sometimes glad I had not served Him more. I felt He owed me better than what I was getting, so why should I live for Him? It didn't wash, though. All the while I knew that I was wrong and that I should go back to Him. I deeply wanted to have the courage to return to full joy in Jesus.

I never made fun of the church, as some of my friends and relatives did. I knew better than that. But I went sparingly to the Brethren chapel in my grandparents' town, and then only to please my born-again grandmother. I went late and left early, sitting in a back row, doing my best to appear uninterested. It wasn't difficult.

I worked part-time for my British grandfather in his small business of selling sauces and smoked fish to restaurants. When my last year of St. Alban's was over, I considered myself a real British man of the world. My six or eight friends from the neighborhood were from slightly outside the circle of my British contacts, but that just made me feel more important.

I joined the local university club and bought myself a pipe, unconsciously imitating Mr. Thompson, my old art teacher. I studied a Dale Carnegie book and learned "how to win friends and influence people," by talking all the time about the other person's interests and point of view and acting interested in any small detail about his or her life. I was a fast-talking, smooth-working phony, and inside I hated myself.

My friends, though non-Christians, were really super kids. By most standards, they were straight. They never got drunk, though they drank a little. And what I considered sins—going to soccer games on Sundays, fantasizing about girls, and wasting time—were about the worst things they did.

They danced, too, but dancing embarrassed me—I felt awkward. I used those friends as an excuse to be more worldly than my conscience was comfortable with, but it wouldn't be fair to say they were bad influences on me. Instead, I missed my opportunity to be a good influence on them. If I had been able to communicate what the Lord could do for them at that stage in their lives, it might have made all the difference in the world.

But I wanted to be "in." I wanted to be "cool." I didn't want them to think I was peculiar. The fear of the Lord kept me from going off the deep end and into any gross sin. Still, I was far from the Lord and ashamed to stand up for Him. In later years, after I got back into fellowship with God, the memory of the way I shamed the Lord then was a big source of guilt for me.

The turning point came just before Carnival Week.

6

Carnival Week in most of Latin America is similar to Mardi Gras in New Orleans, only more wild. It's a week of total abandonment. Any business that isn't crucial to the festivities is closed for the whole week. It's the week before Lent and is followed by forty days of confession and penance, so, during the carnival, *anything* goes.

People dress in costumes and masks and dance around the clock. It's not unusual for a young person to experience his first night of drunkenness—or worse—during Carnival Week.

I had grown tired of the sophisticated little parties and games the university club offered, so doing something more bizarre with my other friends at first sounded like an exciting alternative. We made big plans for celebrating Carnival Week of 1952. The more I thought about it, however, the more ominous it became.

Somehow I felt if I got involved in Carnival, I could be severing my relationship with the Lord. I had already been ignoring God's ownership of my life and soul. While in my head I knew that nothing could separate me from the love of Christ, in my heart I feared God might not forgive this out-and-out mockery of everything I had been taught.

What would happen if something snapped within me and I went off the deep end at a wild party? All of the supposed fun I had been having for months left me bored. Somehow I knew if I went to Carnival Week, temptation would overwhelm me and I would be engulfed in sin. I knew my mother and other Christian relatives prayed daily that I would walk with the Lord again, and the more I thought about it the more panicky I became.

I had to get out of Carnival Week, or I would be swallowed up, finished, sunk. I'm sure the Holy Spirit was convicting me. Toying with the world was one thing, but abandoning self-respect and flaunting God's law was something else. I wanted no part of it.

There was no purpose in my life, nothing to look forward to except more of the same "fun." If I went to Carnival Week, I was convinced

I would have gone beyond the point of no return, humanly speaking. I had to get out of it.

To make matters worse, my grandparents were gone that weekend and the house was empty. I was all on my own. The next day my friends would come by to pick me up for the first day of the week-long Carnival festivities. I was beside myself. There was no way I had the strength to simply tell them I wasn't going. I had to have a reason.

Dedicated to God again

Falling to my knees by my bed, I pleaded with God: "Get me out of this and I will give up everything that's of the world. I will serve You and give my whole life to You. Just get me out of this!"

God must have a good sense of humor. The next morning I awoke on my back, staring at the ceiling. Slowly I sat up, swung my legs over the side of the bed, and sat there a moment. I yawned. My mouth felt strange. I touched it. I felt no pain, but it was bloated.

I stumbled to the mirror. My mouth was so swollen it looked as if I had a ping-pong ball in it. Staring straight into the reflection of my own eyes, I worked up a crooked smile. I looked like I had just come home from the dentist. "God has answered my prayer!" I said aloud.

I called up one of my friends. "I can't go to the dance tonight, and I won't be going to the carnival at all this week."

"Come on, Luis! Everything has been planned!"

"No. I have a good reason, and I will not go."

"I'm coming over," he insisted. "You must be crazy."

A few minutes later he showed up with three or four other guys and girls. They insisted that the swelling would go down and that I should change my mind, but by then I had a full head of steam going, and I resisted until they left, puzzled and angry that I had let the gang down. It was the beginning of the end of my relationship with them. I didn't leave them; they left me.

I should have told them that, because of my faith in the Lord Jesus, I was afraid of the sin in which I might get involved. I should have winsomely sought to lead them to Christ. But I was so spiritually bankrupt then that it took that fat lip to deliver me.

Knowing how good the Gospel is, I am ashamed I was so cowardly. But at least I had made my decision, taken my stand, and broken with the world. I went back into the house, broke my pipe in two, tore up my university club membership card, and ripped up all my soccer and car-racing magazines and many record albums.

The next day I went to church morning and night. The rest of the town, it seemed, was frolicking in sin. I was glad to have escaped. Everything changed that weekend. I was excited. Life perked up and had meaning again.

Looking back, I'm so thankful for the promise of Philippians 1:6, which says: "I am sure that God who began the good work within you will keep right on helping you grow in his grace until his task within you is finally finished on that day when Jesus Christ returns" (TLB).

Slowly I was seeing that, although I might fail God many times in my life, He would never fail me. Just as the Lord Jesus never gave up on Simon Peter, I would learn, step by step, what it meant to live a godly life.

I bought myself a new Bible, intentionally choosing one published in Spanish. I wanted to get out of the proud little world of people who thought they were superior because they were better educated and bilingual and more well-to-do. That was a difficult move for me to make, particularly because everything from the Bible and anything else of a spiritual nature had come to me in English.

Working at the Bank of London

It was time to start a career in which I could draw a good salary and help support my mother and sisters. Because I had been successful in my math and business courses, one of my former professors recommended the Bank of London, a huge, block-long complex near the heart of the capital, with several buildings and more than five hundred employees.

My British education and bilingual abilities made me attractive to the Bank of London, and I was hired as a junior employee in training, at a decent salary for someone my age. I loved being a working man, traveling on the subway, dressing up, and working in the sophisticated, bustling metropolis. Buenos Aires had 5 million residents back then. It looked a lot like Paris with its boulevards, sidewalk cafes, and beautiful people.

Working there could have made it more difficult to break away from the style of life I now despised. The bank was full of office politics, the old-boy system, golf, tennis, rugby, cricket, card games, drinking, parties, and all the rest. But those things irritated me now.

I wanted nothing to do with them. The pendulum had swung completely back.

Having tasted what the world has to offer, I wanted no more. With my family living hand-to-mouth in Cordoba, several hundred miles north, I had more important concerns. I dreamed of perhaps becoming a lawyer, of changing Argentina, of making all of South America a decent place for troubled, poor people to live without getting walked on.

I could discuss the subject for hours, and my friends and relatives warned me I was taking life too seriously. Perhaps I was, but I didn't think so. How could people play and party and carry on, when others were going broke and being cheated and living in poverty? How could they ignore the lower class, when widows and orphans were begging for help?

I was looking for the best way to change my world. I wasn't sure banking was it, though I loved it in many respects. I was learning more than I ever had in such a short time, and I was a go-getter. When my own work was done, I went to the people above my level in different departments, peppering them with questions about every aspect of their jobs and causing them to be suspicious of my ambitions.

I read the banking manuals in Spanish and English, learning the international banking system from A to Z. Those were heady days. I was full of big dreams.

My best memories from that brief period revolve around the walks and talks I had with my uncle, Jack Balfour. We lived in the same house, and after I broke with my worldly friends, he and I would take trips into the night and walk around. We talked for hours. He was very spiritual, and just five years older than I was. He still is the epitome of humility and was one of my closest friends.

Argentine cities were exciting in those days. Thousands and thousands of families jammed the walkways and shops, even as late as midnight. There was music and laughter and the smell of food. Jack and I talked of what we would do to change the world. He was a writer, so we dreamed up a Christian magazine and even made mock-up dummies of the cover and page layouts.

Much of what we talked about and planned for the publication I saw become reality years later when we launched *Continente Nuevo*, the first truly international, interdenominational magazine for pastors and other Christian leaders throughout the Spanish-speaking world.

From the start, our goal in publishing *Continente Nuevo* has been to "feed the shepherds who feed the flock of God." Each issue focuses on a single theme: the authority of the Bible, for example, or pastoral prayer, or dealing with the cults. More than 40,000 leaders ask to receive each issue. Many write to tell us what an encouragement it is to them—the response is far more enthusiastic than Jack and I could have ever dreamed.

I was full of idealism and ambition in those days. From my study of John 14:12-15, for instance, I began to discover the importance of dreaming great dreams, planning great plans, praying great prayers, and obeying God's great commands.

There were so many things I wanted to see happen, things I wanted to do. I recalled President Abraham Lincoln's remark, "I shall prepare, and one day my chance will come." I was convinced of that. I wanted to learn, to develop, to make a difference in society. But first, I wanted to help my own family.

The best way to do that, in my opinion, was to move north four hundred miles to Cordoba where the Bank of London had a branch office. There I could be with my family, start over socially, and get my roots deep into a good, solid local church.

I already had received a couple of promotions at work, mostly because I was bilingual. I was doing all right with a little desk job, but it was time for me to move.

Asking for a transfer

I knew I would probably be laughed out of the office, or even fired, but I got up the nerve to stop by the personnel department. Asking for a transfer simply wasn't done, but I had worked myself into such a frenzy over the state of the world and especially my own spiritual condition, that it didn't matter. I would have to take that chance.

I filled out an application for transfer and sent it back to the personnel office. To me it was a spiritual decision. I would not have been surprised if they had fired me. If that was God's way of getting me out of a situation He didn't want me in, I was willing to accept it.

I called my mother and told her I had decided to follow the Lord. I also mentioned the application I had submitted at work. I couldn't promise it would mean a move to Cordoba, but she was thrilled anyway and no doubt started praying for just that.

When I received a memo, asking that I report to the personnel office, my resolve nearly went out the window. *What a fool*, I told myself. *You've been an idiot! These people have been good to you, and now you ask to be transferred to some remote branch office!*

Then I found myself shifting into the spiritual thought patterns learned from my mother, and my resolve returned. Even if the firing was painful and I had been stupid, I decided it was a sacrifice for the Lord, and He would provide.

7

W hy do you want to transfer to Cordoba?" the personnel
manager asked me.

I told him that it was because my mother and sisters lived
there and needed me, and that I knew Cordoba had a good branch
bank. I waited in silence for his decision.

"You know," he said, "it would be good for you. With a branch of
that size, you can learn banking more quickly since there are only
one or two people in each major department. There won't be a jungle
of people to go around.

"In fact, we'll put this down as if it were our idea, and then we can
justify paying for your move and giving you a promotion and raise."

I was flabbergasted. But he wasn't finished.

"If you progress as nicely there as you have here at headquarters,
within six months we'll put you in charge of foreign operations of
that branch, and in a year we'll bring you back here for a few weeks
of specialized training. In our eyes, you will begin as the number four
man in Cordoba."

I was not yet eighteen years old.

Radio ministry

A few weeks before leaving, I was lying on the living-room floor
at my Uncle Arnold's and Aunt Marjorie's home, listening to a
short-wave HCJB radio program from Quito, Ecuador. I didn't hear
the preacher's name, but I heard him exhorting and calling men to
come to Jesus Christ in a vibrant, somewhat high-pitched and excited
voice. Then I heard a man's strong, deep voice, singing a song by
William T. Sleeper:

> Out of my bondage, sorrow and night,
> Jesus, I come, Jesus, I come;
> Into Thy freedom, gladness and light,

Jesus, I come to Thee.
Out of my sickness into Thy health,
  Out of my want and into Thy wealth,
  Out of my sin and into Thyself,
Jesus, I come to Thee.

The whole program left me exhilarated. Later I realized I had been listening to Billy Graham and George Beverly Shea.

Stretched out on that living-room floor, I prayed: "Jesus, someday use me on the radio to bring others to You, just as this program has firmed up my resolve to completely live for You."

Little did I know that one day I would preach to tens of millions of people via HCJB, Far East Broadcasting Company, Moody Broadcasting, Trans World Radio, and hundreds of other Christian radio networks and stations here in America and around the world. That youthful prayer has been answered by the Lord more than fully.

I've always believed that big doors turn on small hinges. The story of my life and ministry has turned on a lot of small hinges over the years, but one of the most important ones, by God's grace, was my move to Cordoba. It changed me. I became a different person.

I had been through a lot of new beginnings before, but this time I was taking charge of the family. My mother's influence on me would again be for the best. I would find it easier to live for God in a Christian home where that was expected and encouraged.

We were a big family, but we rented a small house because there was little money. My very good salary didn't go far. Once in a while some old business debt would be paid by someone honest enough to look up my mother and take care of it, but otherwise we had no money for anything beside the absolute essentials.

In Cordoba, banking became secondary to me. First and foremost was the family, and soon after I arrived I dived right into the middle of the local Christian Brethren assembly.

Christian discipleship

It was a group of about one hundred thirty people, probably one of the biggest local churches I had ever seen. They had an exciting program, run totally by the elders and the one full-time missionary, George Mereshian. He took me under his wing immediately after I expressed a desire to be baptized by immersion and become active in the work.

This was a very strict and doctrinally sound church, and they held fast to the rule that a person could not participate in ministry leadership roles unless he had been baptized, served in lesser capacities, and studied God's Word in-depth for several years.

The Bible teaching program was so sound and systematic that it was like attending a seminary. I began to devour commentaries and supplementary books by great Christian preachers, teachers, and writers. Biographies of evangelists Martin Luther, John Calvin, George Whitefield, John Wesley, D. L. Moody, Charles E. Finney, George Müller, and Billy Sunday, and books by Bible teachers Oswald Chambers, C. H. Mackintosh, F. B. Meyer, J. I. Packer, S. I. Ridout, Oswald J. Smith, C. H. Spurgeon, and scores of others influenced my life and ministry.

Many of these were rare copies of out-of-print editions, loaned to me by missionaries and national Christian leaders. Today, especially when I'm in Great Britain, I eagerly comb the used-book stores, in search of more of these precious treasures to add to my already rather full library.

You'll find many of the volumes I've collected heavily underlined with little notes in the margins. I try to take especially good notes when reading biographies. My one hobby, if I have any, is studying church history. There are so many practical lessons to learn.

I worked harder at my Bible study program than I did at the bank—not because I was lazy at work, but because I quickly learned how to fulfill my responsibilities and moved up fast. When I landed the foreign-operations job, I found I could get my work done in a few hours and have the rest of the time to study my Bible and commentaries, with total permission from my supervisors.

One Sunday in church we sang the hymn, "Am I a Soldier of the Cross?" I sang with the enthusiasm the tempo demands, but at first hardly thought about the words. The Lord must have used all the Bible knowledge that was being poured into me to make me sensitive to Him, because suddenly I was overcome with the meaning of the song.

> Am I a soldier of the cross?
> A foll'wer of the Lamb?
> And shall I fear to own His cause
> Or blush to speak His name?

The lyrics by Isaac Watts burst into my mind as if God Himself was impressing an exhortation on my heart. "You sing of being a soldier of the cross, and yet you do nothing," He seemed to say. "You have never suffered for Me; no one has ever said a thing to you against God. Think of Mildred Cable and Francesca French—those two missionary ladies from Asia, whom your mother read to you about and whom you met several years ago."

My thoughts turned to those early years of cowardice back in Buenos Aires and how little I was doing even now, compared to those inspiring women. I could hardly continue singing. *What kind of soldier are you?* I asked myself. *When were you ever dragged by the hair or stoned or spat upon for the Gospel? You stand here and sing about being a soldier of the cross, but you are no soldier yet.*

That rebuke did me good. I began to realize that all this Bible study and training under the elders and Mr. Mereshian was a call from the Lord to serve Him and even suffer for Him, if necessary.

At this point I knew I probably wouldn't be a banker all my life. And I wouldn't be a lawyer or a judge, either. I couldn't change my nation or the world through finances or law or politics or sociology or psychology. I was going to have to become a soldier of the cross or quit singing about it.

Spiritual struggles

I had consecrated my life to Christ, all right. But was I totally committed to choosing His will over and against my own? It was a struggle, make no mistake about it.

I remember wrestling in prayer with the Lord over the course of several weeks and months. I felt God was asking if I would be willing to do anything for Him. I wanted to say "yes," but I couldn't. I was afraid the Lord would ask me to be a missionary to lepers in Africa, where I'd end up contracting the disease myself.

I could almost see the white spots starting to appear on my hands and face! Sermon illustrations I'd heard about leprosy had scared the wits out of me. So I'd get up from my knees, shaken, holding back from the Lord in this one area.

I felt the Lord was saying, "Listen, Luis, it's either all or nothing. Are you willing to do *anything* for Me?"

Kneeling by my bed one Saturday, I finally said, "Lord, yes, if it has to be, I'll even be a leper, for Your name's sake."

A few Sundays later, it was time for my baptism. As a baptismal day gift, my mother gave me my own copy of C. H. Spurgeon's *Lectures to My Students*, a book on preaching and pastoral work for young preachers. That book molded my young life and has marked my ministry.

That night, after re-reading part of Spurgeon's book and dreaming of the day I'd begin preaching there in Cordoba, I went to bed all excited about what God had in store for me in the days ahead.

About midnight, however, I woke up with the most frightful doubts about my own salvation! I panicked, worried I might not be a true believer, after all. Only by crying out to the Lord in prayer and listening to my mother's wise and scriptural words did I regain a sense of His peace and assurance that all truly was well with my soul, thanks to Jesus' work on the cross on my behalf.

Only later did I discover that Satan often viciously attacks us both before *and* immediately after a significant spiritual breakthrough. If we consecrate ourselves, despite Satan's furious objections, he can't resist swinging one last dirty punch to try to knock us out of the saddle.

That wouldn't be the last time Satan tried to use one of his rotten schemes to stamp me out.

8

After my baptism, I no longer was restricted from any ministerial activity with which I wanted to help. I soon joined George Mereshian and others when they went out to do evangelistic street meetings. Someone would start singing and playing an instrument to draw a crowd, while Mr. Mereshian tried to find an electrical outlet for his audio equipment.

He was quite a salesman. He always managed to charm people into letting him use a wall outlet in their house. Then we were in business.

My first speaking engagement, if I remember right, was at one of those street meetings. Those meetings can fizzle fast if they're not kept lively. I was nervous, but I had prepared for days and was more worried about keeping the crowd there than about whether I was saying everything just right.

A close friend and I really started enjoying the street meetings. He was the better speaker and could always get the crowd excited. He had a lot of zeal. It was great to plan for those little junkets together.

Although we saw few conversions, I began to learn the basics of evangelism. We ran into everything: laughter, scorn, questions that required quick answers, questions that required diplomacy, you name it.

One thing the elders burned into our minds was that we had the truth. We stood on the truth. Let people argue and heckle all they want. Truth is truth, and any honest person who hears it knows it.

First sermon

The first time I formally spoke in church was at a youth meeting, which customarily was attended by the adults, as well. There was a crowd of 120, including my beaming relatives. I was scared to death.

I had studied Spurgeon's notes on Psalm 1 from *The Treasury of David* for weeks on my knees. And I had prayed and prayed. Knowing that almost everyone in the audience was at least as accomplished

---

a Bible student as I this speaking engagement more frightening than preaching on the street.

Out on the streets, I could preach my heart out. Why was I so nervous this time? Years later, Billy Graham explained: If you can quote a few verses of Scripture, the average unchurched Joe thinks you're a theological genius. Thus, the street meetings were simpler—my audiences out there weren't theologically critical, for the most part.

In the assembly of believers, however, I had to do more than quote a few verses from Psalm 1. The congregation was expecting a message from God—which it was—though it came through my lips and Spurgeon's pen. Still, God had impressed it upon me to preach it, too.

I thought I was ready, but I dreaded going through with it. What if I didn't say something exactly right? I'd instantly see it in their eyes.

It was all I could do to talk myself into showing up, but I had my outlines and notes prepared. I figured I had at least forty minutes of thoughts and hoped I wouldn't go over my time allotment.

I needn't have worried. My throat was dry. The butterflies never stopped. I practically read my notes verbatim and finished in less than twelve minutes.

I felt I had failed, even though Spurgeon's thoughts were good. More than anything, I was relieved it was over for now.

Financial struggles

Meanwhile, the financial situation at home wasn't getting any better. The Lord had impressed upon me to take care of my mother and sisters; He would take care of me. And He did, even though we sometimes ate a loaf of French bread and a little garlic for our whole meal, and I wore my Uncle Arnold's discarded suits and my grandfather's old topcoats.

That didn't bother me. I was in the Word and had shaken many of my fears of not being accepted or part of the crowd. I had read about the suffering George Müller and other outstanding Christians had gone through. This was nothing in comparison. So I worked hard at the bank and kept advancing, but still the money never stretched very far.

I knew God meant it for our good. We had been wealthy, so our poverty was a valuable education. The experience taught me to walk humbly before the Lord and to look to Him for everything. There was nowhere else for us to look.

The Lord's words became a daily reality to us: "But seek first his kingdom and his righteousness, and all these things will be given to you as well" (Matthew 6:33).

I now feel I better understand and more deeply care about the poor because I've been there. As a result, my family and evangelistic team make it a priority to do what we can—individually and working with others—to help widows, orphans, and others in need here in the States and around the world.

Diligent study, service

At the bank my co-workers began to call me "Pastor." I found still more and more time, even at the office, to study theology. I studied whole books of the Bible, using works like *Jeremiah* by F. B. Meyer. I read through Bible dictionaries and commentaries such as Jamieson, Fausset, and Brown on the New Testament. I often studied several different subjects a day.

I couldn't have studied more or harder if I had been in seminary. In a way, I was in seminary. For three years, George Mereshian discipled me three hours a day, three days a week. I learned as much from him as I did from the study itself.

By the time I was in my early twenties, the elders had delegated more and more of the church work to several of us younger men. We held street meetings galore, spoke at little churches all over the countryside, sold Bibles, handed out tracts, visited the sick and elderly, organized a large Sunday school program, led youth meetings, and held all-night prayer meetings. We even developed a seven-minute daily radio program. The church was really hopping!

Though we were far ahead of most people our age in serving the Lord, we desperately needed to know how to rely on the indwelling Christ and not on our own efforts. We felt hot and cold at the same time. The twin temptations of pride and passion were almost unbearable.

We had hoped that our being active Christians would somehow diminish the normal thought-life temptations that face young men. But that just didn't happen. We were expecting more than the Bible promises.

Unfortunately, many of the key men in our young people's group dropped out. Others joined us, but I felt let down that the original core of committed young men broke up after about two years. Why didn't they go the distance?

I weighed the whole matter for several days, seeking the Lord in prayer. I wound up still frustrated, still short of what I felt the Scriptures offer in terms of God's fullness, peace, victory, purity, and the Holy Spirit's overflowing work in and through our lives described in John 7:37-39 and other verses.

No adult converts yet

Equally frustrating, my preaching seemed to have no power. I was prepared, psyched up, prayed up, backed up, and zealous. Yet I saw no immediate fruit, except for a few kids who trusted Christ when I directed and taught Vacation Bible School.

Nothing I did seemed to make any difference. I was inspired by the things I read and heard about other evangelists, but it seemed obvious I didn't have whatever they had, namely the Holy Spirit's power in my life.

Finally I gave God a deadline. If I didn't see any converts by the end of the year, I would quit preaching. Oh, I would still be an active Christian, and I would still read and study and pray and celebrate the Lord's Supper, but I would resign myself to simply assisting others. There was no use preaching evangelistically if no one was coming to Christ.

The end of the year came and went. My mind was made up. I didn't have the gift of evangelism.

On Saturday morning, about four days into the new year, I bought a Spanish translation of Billy Graham's *The Secret of Happiness*, shut the door so I wouldn't be distracted by my younger siblings and their friends, and curled up on the couch to read.

As low as I was, I was blessed by Billy Graham's thoughts on the Beatitudes from Jesus' Sermon on the Mount in Matthew 5. My study habits kicked into gear and I couldn't help but memorize the points he made on each Beatitude.

That night I didn't feel like going to the home Bible study I usually attended, but I caught a bus and went anyway, out of loyalty to the elders. We sang several hymns, but the speaker never showed up.

Finally the man of the house said, "Luis, you're going to have to speak. None of the other preachers are here."

I tried to excuse myself, saying I wasn't prepared and besides, I'd forgotten my Bible.

"Look, there's no one else, Luis. You have to speak."

I hardly had time to breathe a prayer. I borrowed a New Testament, read a Beatitude, repeated a few points I remembered from Billy Graham's book, read another verse, and so on.

Finally I came to the Beatitude, "Blessed are the pure in heart, for they shall see God" (Matthew 5:8 RSV). Suddenly a woman from the neighborhood stood and began to cry. "Somebody help me! My heart is not pure. How am I going to find God?"

I don't remember the woman's name, but I will never forget her words: "Somebody tell me how I can get a pure heart." We went to the Bible and read, "The blood of Jesus, his Son, purifies us from all sin" (1 John 1:7). Before the evening was over, that woman found peace with God and went home with a pure heart overflowing with joy. How delightful it was to lead her to Jesus Christ!

What I learned that evening, of course, was something I had studied and should have known all along: the Holy Spirit does the convicting. I was just a vehicle. God used me in spite of myself, and He did it in His own good time.

As Henrietta Mears said: "To be successful in God's work is to fall in line with His will and do it His way. All that is pleasing to Him is a success."

I ignored the buses that night and walked all the way home, praising the Lord that He had chosen to use me.

9

Others started coming to Jesus Christ through my ministry, first a trickle, then more and more.

Reports of Billy Graham's growing evangelistic ministry began to catch my eye. Friends gave me the book *Revival in Our Time*. It described Graham's 1949 Los Angeles crusade, the event that contributed to what Dr. J. Edwin Orr called the mid-century revival.

Missionaries lent me a dated copy of *Moody Monthly's* report on Billy Graham's 1954 London crusade. What an impact that had on me!

"Why can't we see this in our country?" I wanted to know. A whole nation could be turned around with only a small percentage of conversions. Mass evangelism could lift a nation's moral and ethical standards. History bore that out.

I began to dream that Argentina and eventually all of Latin America could be reached on a large scale for Christ. Here we were working so hard, reaching so few in a massive city of more than 750,000. There had to be a better way to start seeing hundreds and thousands won for Christ. Mass evangelism was the key!

Don't get me wrong. I still believed in one-on-one evangelism. I practice it to this day. I teach it. But eventually it's necessary to move the masses, sway public opinion, influence the thought patterns of the media.

Simply put, a nation will not be changed by timid methods. It must be confronted, challenged, hit with the truth again and again, forcefully, in the power of God's Holy Spirit.

Desire to be an evangelist

The more I prayed and read about mass evangelism, the more convinced I became it was where the Lord wanted me. People wonder if my motivation was at all ego-inspired. In those days, I don't believe I was thinking about making a name for myself.

On the other hand, I accept the biblical sanction of God. I know

Luis Palau

I am ego-centered. From day one I knew if I got out of hand or in the way of God's greater glory, He would quickly put me in my place.

But I also quickly learned I couldn't spend the rest of my life beating my breast and searching my soul. So I simply prayed, "Lord, please make everything I do pleasing to You."

My motivation for personal study shifted into high gear. A Navigators representative to Argentina, Norman Lewis, influenced my life, and memorization became a high priority. Someone else gave me an old Moody correspondence course by Dr. R. A. Torrey, Moody Bible Institute's first superintendent, entitled *How to Work for Christ.* I ate it up. I didn't send the exams to Chicago, but I answered all the questions and memorized almost every verse in the entire eight-volume course.

I organized my days just like a school day, studying one subject for fifty minutes, taking a ten-minute break, then studying another subject. For two years, I studied several hours a day, five days a week.

When I read about this new invention, television, in *Time* magazine, I knew it would eventually play a major role in world evangelization. I was fascinated by the technological and social possibilities of the new medium, even though television was fairly new in the United States and almost nonexistent in Latin America.

It would be years before I preached on television, but I was rehearsing in Cordoba, Argentina, South America, when television was in its infancy. I knew that some day my chance would come, and I wanted to be ready for the Lord to use me for His glory.

During this time I began to envision, during prayer, reaching out to great crowds of people, people by the thousands, stadiums full. It was as real to me as a prophetic word.

At first I didn't know what to make of it. Was it just my imagination telling me I wanted to be a well-known preacher? I decided it wasn't. I believed the Lord was laying on my heart what He was going to do. It had to be the Lord, because I was totally bankrupt of the resources needed to accomplish something like that. I could study and work and pray and do my own little thing there in Cordoba, but, beyond that, I was helpless without a miracle.

Tent meetings

Some of us still-zealous young people were encouraged by the elders to go ahead and buy a tent so we could reach people who wouldn't come to the chapel. We advertised children's meetings in the afternoons and evangelistic rallies in the evenings.

Early on, many of the Christians in the area came to support us and make the unsaved people feel more comfortable in a crowd. It was thrilling to be preaching the Gospel and I knew it was training me for even bigger and better things. They tell me I preached loudly and gestured expansively, as if I had a crowd of 10,000. It got to the point where all I wanted to do was study, pray, preach, and lead more people to Christ.

As I read biographies about evangelists of the past, I paid close attention to how each moved out of his own locality and began preaching to the masses. With one exception, they started as unknowns. For the most part, they had no contacts and no money. They were simply used of God. God did the work through them.

Perhaps there was hope for me, I decided. Just to be involved in a big crusade would have been exciting. I had no idea how soon it would happen.

Having been named general co-secretary of a national youth congress, I was invited to meet Jim Savage, a former Youth for Christ man, president of a seminary, and a representative of the Billy Graham Evangelistic Association. I could hardly believe it. I barely slept nights. Billy Graham was coming to Cordoba in person!

I felt on top of the world. I was gaining entree to larger, wider audiences. And I was bringing well-known speakers and Bible teachers in to speak at different events we organized. Soon, however, I was shocked to find out how many of these men could preach a dynamite message and then turn right around and put down a fellow preacher as soon as they stepped off the platform. I was drawn into the same type of cynicism and backbiting, which quickly led to another roller-coaster experience of guilt for me.

The day finally came when I joined other church leaders to hear Jim Savage speak about the possibility of Billy Graham's coming to Argentina. What impressed me most—besides the crowd (as big as I'd ever seen for any Christian event, and it was just over a thousand)—was a brief film of Graham speaking to Christian leaders in India.

The film revealed an unbelievable crowd, but the dramatic effect the camera left was that Billy was talking directly to us. Early in his message, which was not evangelistic, but directed at Christian leaders, the camera panned the whole crowd to show the tens of thousands.

Yet, when Billy got to the heart of his message, the camera zoomed in close to his face. There on the big screen he stared right into my eyes. He was preaching from Ephesians 5:18, "And do not be drunk with wine, in which is dissipation; but be filled with the Spirit" (NKJV). It was as if the crowd in India didn't exist. He was looking right at me and shouting, "Are you filled with the Spirit? Are you filled with the Spirit? Are you filled with the Spirit?"

Somehow I knew that was my problem. That's what caused my up-and-down Christianity. That's why I had zeal and commitment, but little fruit or victory. I didn't know how to be filled with all the fullness of God Himself. What was the secret? As it turns out, I wouldn't discover the answer until I had been in the United States for six months.

As people began to recognize my bent for evangelism, and speaking engagements became even more frequent, my mother started urging me to leave the bank and pursue full-time ministry.

"Mom, how are you going to live?" I objected. "We have a lot of mouths to feed!"

"Luis, you know if the Lord is in it, He will provide."

"But I don't feel the call," I said. "I don't have that final call that tells me it would be all right."

"The call? What call?" she said. "He gave the commission 2,000 years ago, and you've read it all your life. How many times do you want Him to give the commandment before you obey it? It isn't a question of call; it's a question of obedience. The call He has given; it's the answer He's waiting for."

I feared she was right, but I wasn't confident enough in the Lord to quit my job just yet, even though I was becoming less enamored of banking every day.

Appointment with destiny

One day in late 1958 I received a flier announcing a speaking engagement by two Americans: Dick Hillis, a former missionary to China and prisoner of the communists, and Ray Stedman, a pastor from Palo Alto, California. I was afraid it might be just an anti-communist rally, but I was curious to see a pastor from California.

I went alone to the meeting, and afterward noticed Pastor Stedman standing by himself. I introduced myself in English and was amazed when he immediately asked me a lot of questions and seemed genuinely interested in me.

I told Ray all about myself, my job, my motorbike, and my family. When he invited me to a Bible study with a few missionaries the next morning, I was flattered.

Years later Ray told me that when he first saw me, the Lord impressed upon his heart to see that I got to the United States. He didn't know why and, of course, didn't even know who I was. When he discovered I was actively involved in evangelism, he knew his leading was of God.

The next day after the Bible study I gave Ray a ride into town on my motorbike so he could do some shopping, and we talked some more. "Would you like to go to seminary?" he asked.

"It would be nice, but I'm not sure I'll ever make it. I don't have a lot of money, and my church doesn't encourage formal theological education."

"Well," he said, "it could be arranged if the Lord wanted it." I couldn't argue with that. "How would you like to come to the United States?"

"I've thought about it," I admitted. "Maybe someday I'll be able to go, the Lord willing." I was just shooting the breeze. It never dawned on me a minister from the United States would be able to arrange anything like that. I thought he was just speculating.

"You know, Luis," he responded, "the Lord may just will it."

10

T he next night, after hearing Dick Hillis speak, I saw Dick and Ray Stedman off at the airport. "I'll see you in the United States," Ray said.

"Well, the Lord willing, maybe someday," I said.

"No, Luis, the Lord *is* going to will. I'll write you from the plane."

To me, Ray Stedman seemed like a warm person, flattering, and a bit unrealistic. There was no way I was going to get to the United States within the next decade. It was out of the question. If the ministers there had as little money as the ones in South America, he wouldn't be able to help me. So why even dream?

A few days later, Ray's letter arrived with the news that he knew a businessman who wanted to finance my trip to the United States so I could study at Dallas Theological Seminary. It was a thrill—I had read about the school; its founder, Dr. Lewis Sperry Chafer; president, John Walvoord; and all its wonderful teachers—but I quickly got cold feet.

There was too much to do; I didn't want to spend four more years in school. And who would take care of my family? I wrote Stedman back and thanked him, but declined his offer.

He wrote back quickly, assuring me that someone from the United States would be able to provide for my family, too. It was too incredible. I didn't know how to respond, and because other exciting events began to emerge in my life, I didn't answer his letter for several months.

Procrastination had always been a problem with me, but this was really rude. I simply ignored a couple more letters, and soon my life was busy with decisions and new open doors.

I confronted the bank manager with a few new policies I wasn't comfortable with and told him that, due to my Christian testimony, I wasn't sure I could do everything required of me. Those practices weren't illegal, but they raised some ethical questions.

I knew I was taking my job in my hands, and the manager was not at all pleased. He reminded me of all the bank had done for me and all they had planned for me. Rather than agreeing that some of the practices might be questionable, he insinuated that I was jeopardizing my career by rocking the boat. I knew if push ever came to shove and I was asked to do or say something I didn't feel right about, I would refuse, and that would be that.

My stock in the bank dropped overnight. I was living on borrowed time, and I knew it. No doubt the headquarters bank in Buenos Aires had received a report on me and would begin cultivating a new foreign-operations manager. It didn't take long, however, for me to discover all of this had happened in God's time.

Going into full-time ministry

A few days after my confrontation with the manager, I noticed an American opening a new account. I greeted him in English and struck up a conversation. He was Keith Bentson, representing SEPAL, the Latin American division of OC International, the missions organization Dick Hillis founded and led. I told him I was a Christian, too, and we had a nice chat.

A few days later, when he came in to make his first deposit, Keith mentioned he was looking for a bilingual Christian man who might want to work for SEPAL, translating English material into Spanish for their magazine, La Voz (The Voice).

"You've got your man," I said.

"Who?" Keith asked.

"It's me." As soon as he mentioned the job, I knew it was for me.

"Oh, Luis, you'd better think about it and talk with your family. We're talking about a very, very small salary; no doubt much less than you're making here."

"I'll talk to my family," I promised, "but I'm your man. This is exciting. I'm sure it's of God."

Keith needed time to check me out, too, which ruffled a few feathers at church. The elders didn't like the idea that I would be working with an interdenominational organization. But I already had my mother's blessing and would not be deterred.

My only stipulation was that I be allowed to come in late on Monday mornings. I explained to Keith I had speaking engagements lined up for many Sunday nights to come and wanted to be able to

Luis Palau

fulfill those obligations. Some were as far away as seventy miles, and it was easier to come back the next morning on the bus.

Once we had that out of the way and I got over the shock of the tiny salary offered, I was on cloud nine. I finally had found a way to get into full-time Christian work! I hadn't been so sure about God's leading in my life for a long time.

So, less than a week after my confrontation with the bank manager, I gave him notice. He gave me my final check, asked me to give instructions to my fill-in replacement, and then I was free. Two of my sisters had found jobs by now, so having my salary cut by more than half would not hurt the family much.

I went from being close to the top at the bank to low man at SEPAL. But I loved it. I did a little of everything, including representing the mission at conventions. I continued my tent preaching on my own time, but one of the greatest lessons and blessings of those days came from praying with Keith Bentson.

Lessons in prayer

After I had been at SEPAL a few weeks, Keith asked me to stay at the office after closing time one Wednesday evening. He didn't want other staff members to think I was getting privileged treatment. He simply wanted to pray with me.

That first Wednesday night he prayed for me and my family, then my church and all the elders by name. I was amazed at how informed he was, since he didn't attend our church. It was exciting to hear him pour out his heart, imploring, "Oh, God, bless these men for Your service and Your glory!" It made me want to pray, too, so I did.

The next week Keith brought a map of the city of Cordoba and pinpointed the fifteen or sixteen local churches of the Brethren movement. Then he prayed for each church, literally one by one, by name and address and for the key leaders, if he knew them. It was as if we had taken a trip around the city on our knees.

He just prayed out his soul, teaching me what intercessory prayer was all about. It was thrilling. We got into the habit of praying conversationally, back and forth, and often he paced the room as he talked to the Lord.

The next Wednesday his map of the city included churches of all denominations. He prayed for each one, incredibly knowing the pastor's name, in most cases. By doing that, he confirmed something I had felt for years. I had always wondered why, when we were taught about unity in Christ, that oneness shouldn't include devout Christians of other denominations. Now I was being taught the oneness of the Church through the fervent prayers of this energetic, vibrant, devoted, committed missionary.

The meaning of Ephesians 6:18 began to sink in with enormous strength: "Pray at all times in the Spirit, with all prayer and supplication. To that end keep alert with all perseverance, making supplication for all the saints" (RSV).

As the weeks went by, Keith's map got bigger, first encompassing the province, the nation, then other nations, until finally we had prayed for the whole world.

Those prayer meetings in Keith's office revolutionized my life. My vision for those who needed Christ became international, geographical, global.

All during this time, the tent ministry was growing because my friends and I pulled in people from other churches throughout the city. I dreamed of having an actual evangelistic team, but I had no money, and I didn't know where I was going to draw the talent to help me. One night, it fell into my lap.

First team members

After the tent meeting that night, a handsome and winsome American named Bruce Woodman introduced himself and asked if I needed a soloist and song leader for the meetings. He was a missionary looking for a ministry and was eager to help out. I said sure. He told me he also knew a keyboard man named Bill Fasig, who had worked under New York evangelist Jack Wyrtzen and who could play the organ or piano for us.

Up until that time, our music had been an accordion, played by my sisters or a friend from our local church. Did Bruce and Bill ever make a difference! Bruce was a perfect emcee, song leader, and soloist. He really could get a crowd excited. He did it in the Spirit, too. And of course Bill Fasig has gone on to become a widely known artist and has played for Billy Graham through the years. In my mind, we had just graduated. Now we had a team.

I knew I wasn't that technically great as a speaker, but I kept working at it and studying. I breathed wrong, which made it hard on my voice. But many books by the old-time preachers were full of advice on projection, sermon preparation, and anything else a budding speaker wanted to know. And when Bruce Woodman finally got through to me with counsel on how to breathe from my dia-phragm rather than my throat, he probably added ten years to my speaking voice.

We were busy and happy and productive. Little did we know what was just around the corner. But first I had a rather urgent letter to answer.

11

In my excitement about going into full-time Christian work with SEPAL and finally having my very own evangelistic team, I had put off answering Ray Stedman's increasingly urgent correspondence.

Finally, Ray wrote me a stinging letter, telling me my inaction was irresponsible and rude. He made it clear that if I wanted to come to the United States, I could. I wouldn't be forced to attend Dallas Theological Seminary or stay anywhere else for four years.

I had told Ray one of my big objections was the idea of spending four more years in classes and being almost thirty years old when I finished school. Don't get me wrong. I've taught at Multnomah Biblical Seminary, spoken at dozens of theological institutions here and abroad, and encouraged countless thousands of Christian young people to attend Bible college or seminary. But, for me, time was of the essence, I truly thought.

"Too many people are going to hell for me to be spending four more years reading books," I told Ray. "I can study at home. I'm disciplined, and I enjoy studying. What I need is an opportunity to ask questions of some good Bible teachers and get answers to the really tough ones I haven't been able to resolve through my own reading."

I also wanted to learn more about the United States and what made Americans tick, after all I had read about that exciting country. It was a land of success, and I wanted to know why.

Ray's point, and he was right, of course, was that I should have kept the lines of communication open. That way he could have assured me all my questions would be answered and the obstacles overcome.

He told me there was a one-year graduate course in theology available at Multnomah Biblical Seminary in Portland, Oregon, that might perfectly suit my needs. What's more, I could spend a few months before and after the school year as an intern at his church in

California, together with another young man, Dallas Theological Seminary student Charles Swindoll.

When Ray sent money for my mother, as a token of what they would do while I was there, and also enclosed a check to pay for my trip to Buenos Aires to get my passport, my excuses had run out. I had felt for a long time that God might want me to go to the United States to see more of the world and broaden my understanding, and now the door was wide open. I prayed about it and agreed to go.

Neither the assembly nor SEPAL was terribly excited about it, the latter because they feared I might never return to South America. I got a sermonette about not letting the United States enthrall me: "Your ministry is down here; this is God's will for you, in spite of how attractive the States are."

Little did anyone know then what spheres of ministry God had in store for me throughout Latin America, Europe, Asia, and—eventually—the United States.

I had my first taste of what lay ahead just a few short weeks before departing for seminary.

Church planting

Keith Bentson and my immediate boss, Daniel Ericcson, the editor of *La Voz*, were letting me do more out-of-the-office evangelistic work, including preaching. That, combined with the tent meetings with Bruce Woodman and Bill Fasig, kept me going almost around the clock. I couldn't have been more pleased.

One day, one of SEPAL's newest and most energetic missionaries, Ed Murphy, began laying out an Acts-of-the-Apostles-type strategy for planting a new church where no Christian worker had ever been. The strategy called for taking a team of missionaries and national believers from a nearby town into virgin territory, holding meetings like the apostle Paul, instantly reaping a harvest, discipling them in the basics, and leaving behind an active, functioning New Testament church a few days later.

Ed and the rest of us felt the Lord was calling us to Oncativo, a town of about 12,000 in the province of Cordoba, about fifty miles from the main city. We visited the tiny church in Rio Segundo, one stop earlier along the railroad line, then sent someone to scout out Oncativo. It appeared to be totally pagan. Only one person could recall having ever seen an evangelical or held a tract in his hand—and that some forty years earlier!

Five people from the small church in Rio Segundo agreed to join our church planting team. When we arrived in Oncativo, the three Americans with us—Ed Murphy, Keith Bentson, and Bruce Woodman—caused a lot of excitement. However, they let us nationals carry the ball.

First we asked one of the Oncativo town council leaders if we could participate in the May 25 national celebration and parade, and then say a few words to the people. He turned us down. We then asked if our musicians could join the parade and play some national songs. He turned us down again.

Strangely, we weren't discouraged in the least. To us nationals, even making such bold requests was something new and exhilarating. We weren't going to fear rejection; we were going to plunge in. Finally, we asked around for any foreigners, figuring they would be more open to welcoming us to the city.

We were directed to a Swiss family who for years had run a print shop in town. They welcomed us and, after some discussion, offered us the use of their storage room off the print shop for our meetings.

While eating with them and sharing our mission, the Spirit especially began to work on the heart of the middle-aged, unmarried daughter of the house. She was obviously searching for God and was moved by what we had to say. She became the first convert that week, receiving Christ right at the dinner table! We thought of Lydia mentioned in Acts 16:14, whose heart the Lord opened.

First public invitation

We held an impromptu rally in a park on May 25, handed out hundreds of fliers announcing our meetings, then prayed like crazy that at least a small group would show up. The storage room only could hold about seventy-five people, and that night it was packed. I could hardly wait to preach, especially knowing I would be giving my first bona fide public invitation for people to publicly confess Jesus Christ.

The elders at my church in Cordoba had always discouraged me from using such an "emotional technique." As we had been praying that day, however, I had such a strong urge to give a public invitation that I felt I would be disobeying the Lord to ignore such a clear-cut prompting.

That night I preached on John 10:28-29, one of my favorite passages of Scripture. In it, Jesus gives these word of assurance:

"I give them eternal life, and they shall never perish; no one can snatch them out of my hand. My Father, who has given them to me, is greater than all; no one can snatch them out of my Father's hand."

As I neared the end of my sermon, I was surprised by the unusual freedom I felt to invite people to receive Jesus Christ publicly. It was the first of thousands of similar invitations I would give over the next three and a half decades.

I asked everyone to bow their heads and pray along with me if they wanted to receive Jesus Christ. I then asked for those who had prayed with me to raise their hands to signify their decision. I counted almost three dozen hands and nearly panicked.

So the critics are right! It is all emotion. These invitations are unfair. The people feel pressured; their emotions have been tampered with. I asked people to lower their hands.

"Let me explain again," I said, and I spent another half hour on the passage, clarifying every point, making sure they understood the significance of choosing life with Christ. We prayed again, and I asked for hands. Even more went up!

We held meetings every night and trained the new converts so they could start their own church when we left. By the end of the week, seventy people had professed faith in Jesus Christ.

We didn't have to worry about leaving these brand-new Christians to flounder in their faith. Besides teaching them everything we could in a week—about baptism, communion, witnessing, music, being elders, and preaching the Word—our friends from Rio Segundo had been revived themselves. I knew they would be watching over the new church as if it were made up of their own sons and daughters.

Over the next couple of years, the churches in Rio Segundo and Oncativo multiplied themselves by planting several churches in other nearby towns, proving Ed Murphy and Dick Hillis right: With a lot of work in the power of the Holy Spirit and with the blessing of God, indigenous churches would spring up.

I hardly had time to come down from that experience when it was time for me to leave for the United States. Keith Bentson and some others felt it was my duty to stay in Cordoba. Ed Murphy felt we were on the threshold of revival and wanted to evangelize other towns, without delay. But he also reluctantly admitted it would be helpful for me to go to seminary for a year.

One evening we got together at the Bentsons' to discuss the situation. My mother was firm in her convictions: "I feel this invitation for Luis is of the Lord. I believe he should go to study the Bible in the United States. I'm behind it one hundred percent." In the end, Keith and Ed agreed I could go, but insisted I should come back as soon as possible.

Flying to America

Family members and friends saw me off at the Ezeiza International Airport in Buenos Aires for the first airline flight of my life. It was a tearful farewell, and my mother just couldn't get enough advice into the last few minutes we had left.

As I was pulling away from her in my one-and-only brand-new black suit, she said, "Don't go into the cities, don't travel alone, watch out, don't get shot and stuffed into a trunk, and remember Hebrews thirteen, five and six!" She was worried about murder. I could only think of my imminent trip.

The flight was horrible. The old DC-6 chugged over the Andes mountains, then settled in at a lower altitude to take the strain off the engines. I got nervous and had a stomachache every time the plane climbed or suddenly dropped altitude.

As we flew over the Caribbean at about twenty thousand feet I was thrilled. "Look at all those little white boats," I said in my best English.

My seatmate roused and leaned across to look. "Those are clouds, kid," he said.

By the time we finally arrived in Miami, ten hours later than expected, I'd missed my connecting flight. I was exhausted. My new suit was a shambles. And, clear across the continent, Ray was expecting me to speak at his church the next day!

12

A fter a collect call to Ray Stedman and a restless attempt at getting a few hours sleep, I was finally on my way to San Francisco on a Delta jet. Now that was living! The airline gave away so many free cups of coffee, sugar, plastic spoons, maps, and postcards I couldn't believe it.

As I flew across the United States, stopping over in Atlanta and passing many other great cities, I began to think, *Someday we'll have evangelistic crusades here.* This was only a dream, of course, because I had never even seen a crusade, let alone preached in one yet. But my experience in Oncativo, everything I had read, and the burden God had put on my heart convinced me it was only a matter of time.

By the time Ray's wife, Elaine, met me at the airport in San Francisco, I was a wreck. I was exhausted, clutching a single suitcase and still wearing my tailored black suit, which didn't look so new anymore and definitely looked out of place in laid-back California. Worse, I was going through the first pangs of culture shock and having second thoughts about why I had come to America.

After a few quick reassuring words of greeting, Elaine raced me out to the car and twenty-five miles down the Bayshore Freeway to the Sunday evening service at Peninsula Bible Church in Palo Alto. And I do mean race! We rushed into church after the service had already started, and I was marched right down the aisle and onto the platform next to Ray, to the welcoming applause of the congregation.

Warmly welcomed

Who knows what I said that night or what first impressions I made. All I remember is how warmly I was welcomed, black suit, accent, and all.

Twenty years later, *National Geographic* ran an article about Hispanics coming "to an America that has not always received them gladly." But I found Americans cordial, friendly, interested in getting to know me, and helpful at every turn.

Not that I was the perfect guest. I don't know how the Stedmans put up with me those first few weeks. Within a week I had a horrible toothache to go along with my homesickness. A dentist pulled three teeth and couldn't stop the bleeding for a week, until they diagnosed that I had a vitamin deficiency.

At least having my mouth stuffed with tea bags—and whatever other home remedies they thought might help—kept me from debating with Ray, Elaine, or anyone else who tried to talk to me. For some reason, I was in an argumentative mood and wanted to discuss theology and doctrine for hours.

I had come to the States to learn, but maybe I wasn't yet ready to admit that I didn't have all the answers. Ray and Elaine and their four daughters were so patient and understanding that their harmony pervaded the place, in spite of the fiery Latin who had invaded. Ray's humor kept everyone happy, and we all became fast friends.

Ray became like a father to me and even took to calling me his son when introducing me. He treated me like a son, too, mixing a lot of advice, counsel, and even reprimand, with his friendship.

I've never forgotten the lessons I learned from Ray, just from living with him and watching his life. First was his complete lack of a critical attitude. Another lesson was his extreme patience under pressure. Third, I was touched by his tremendous reliance on the power of Jesus Christ. I also was impressed by his expository preaching and his uninhibited, manly wit and humor.

Mostly, I was impressed that Ray was the same at home as behind the pulpit. Either he never let his hair down, or he always did. There was nothing hidden, no secret life. He was a great role model and encouragement.

He often would say, "If your reputation is OK with the Lord, it's bound to be all right with others. And if it isn't OK with the Lord, it doesn't matter, anyway."

Befriending top politicians

That summer I also learned a valuable lesson from a visiting speaker from India. He was a high government official, and I wanted to find out from him the best technique for getting near presidents and other government leaders. "What's the method?" I asked. "What technique do you use?"

He put his arm around me and smiled. "Young man," he said, "there are no techniques. You must just love them." At first I thought he was putting me on, withholding his secret. I have since learned his were some of the wisest words and counsel I've ever received.

I have met with leaders from all over the world since that time. Sometimes I'm tempted to slip into persuasive methods or political and diplomatic protocol before I remember that what they need most and respond to fastest is love.

Sharing the love and claims of Jesus Christ with government leaders is one of the unique aspects of our ministry. Through the years, members of royalty, presidents, cabinet members, diplomats, congressmen, parliamentarians, and others have listened as we've opened God's Word and shared the Gospel. "Pray for me," they often ask. "I need it."

Such leaders, because of the pressures of their positions and the types of lives they feel they must lead to appear successful, seldom feel genuinely loved. Many of them shed tears when I say I want to pray for them, no strings attached.

I believe if God takes hold of the hearts and lives of a nation's leaders, that nation can be opened to the Gospel and eventually be turned around to the glory of God. We've seen tremendous openings in country after country.

Starting seminary

Two months with the Stedmans wasn't enough time to learn American culture—how to chat and eat and behave the way the natives do—but it was all I had before traveling north to Multnomah Biblical Seminary in Portland, Oregon.

Multnomah was and is a very demanding school, and I found the first semester particularly rough. I had done a lot of reading and studying, but little on biblical anthropology and the doctrine of the indwelling Christ. And that's what I needed.

I was still struggling to find more fruit in my personal spiritual life. I was frustrated in not being able to live out the life-style I saw in men like Ray Stedman and several others at Peninsula Bible Church where he pastored. Their lives exhibited a joy and release and freedom I found attractive. The more I wanted a similar life-style, the more elusive it became.

I was treated royally at Multnomah. The other students were nice and thought I was a friendly, winsome, somewhat different South American. They couldn't have imagined the spiritual battles I was having. If I hadn't cared so much about serving Christ and preaching the Gospel, I might have given it up that first semester and gone back to Cordoba, Argentina.

I was a sincere hypocrite. People always laugh when I say that, but I truly was, and it wasn't funny. Some hypocrites know they are hypocrites and want to be that way. They want to have two lives: one to show off at church and one to live in private. I simply wanted to be the person people thought I was.

If I were to describe myself in those days, I would have to say I was envious, jealous, too preoccupied and self-centered, and ambitious to a wrong degree. No amount of wrestling with myself would rid me of these sins. And yet I tried. I knew it was terrible, but I felt despicable; I hated the idea that I was a hypocrite.

Ready to quit

I hit a new low around Thanksgiving. A friend of Ray Stedman's had paid for my first semester, but wished to remain anonymous. With the second semester only about a month away, I decided it was hopeless to dream anyone would give me ten dollars, let alone pay for another half a year of seminary. *As soon as the term is over, I'm going back to Argentina*, I decided. My mind was made up.

That weekend, I checked my campus mailbox for a letter from home. The only thing in the box was a plain envelope with my name on it. I assumed it was a graded paper.

It was a note: there was no letterhead, it was unsigned, and it was typed. There was no way to tell who it was from. It read:

Dear Luis,

You have been a great blessing to many of us here in the States, and we appreciate what you have taught us. We feel that you deserve help to finish your year at Multnomah; therefore, all your tuition and books have been paid for.

Just check in at the business office, and they will finalize the papers. So you will be grateful to every American you have met or will ever meet, we remain anonymous.

So God was still with me after all! Even with the defeat and frustration I was feeling, God wanted me to know He was there and to hang in and stay at seminary. He had even more good things planned for me, all during the next few weeks.

Meeting Patricia

The first was that I met Patricia Scofield. Actually I had met her earlier in the semester in a group situation, but one evening several of us went to a class party together. For some reason I said to Pat, "Can I walk you over?"

She said, "Sure." It was no big deal. We weren't even together at the party, but I became interested. She seemed mature and smart, knew how to dress well, and in conversation I discovered that she was very spiritually sensitive. I don't know what Pat thought of me at first—she still won't tell me—but I began to look for her on campus.

Pat finally caught on that I was interested, and we saw a lot of each other. There was nothing serious between us yet, but I certainly hoped there would be. I had been smitten, and when I learned that she was going away over the Christmas break and had a few stops to make, I worried one of those stops might be to see an old boyfriend. So I let her know how I felt. It wasn't anything dramatic or romantic, just my usual, straight-out Latin style. I wanted her to know that she was special to me, that I cared for her a great deal, and that I hoped we could spend a lot more time together after the holidays.

13

For one of the last Multnomah chapel services before Pat and I went our separate ways for Christmas break, our speaker was Major Ian Thomas, founder and general director of the Torchbearers, the group that runs the Capernwray Hall Bible School in England.

It was a challenge to make out all his words through a thick British accent and staccato delivery, but I had an edge on the rest of the students. And when Major Thomas spoke and pointed a finger that had been partially cut off, I was intrigued.

Now here's an interesting man, I thought, probably just because he wasn't afraid to use that finger for gesturing. But as soon as he had me hooked, his short message spoke to me. I had been so hungry for answers that I had quit wondering where they would come from. I had all but given up, but, in twenty-two minutes, Ian Thomas got through to me.

His theme was "Any old bush will do, as long as God is in the bush." The essence was that it took Moses forty years in the wilderness to realize that he was nothing. Thomas said God was trying to tell Moses, "I don't need a pretty bush or an educated bush or an eloquent bush. Any old bush will do, as long as I am in the bush. If I am going to use you, I am going to use you. It will not be you doing something for Me, but Me doing something through you."

Thomas said the burning bush in the desert was likely a dry bunch of ugly little sticks that had hardly developed, yet Moses had to take off his shoes. Why? Because this was holy ground. Why? Because God was in the bush!

Learning to depend on God

I realized I was that kind of bush: a worthless, useless bunch of dried-up old sticks. I could do nothing for God. All my reading and studying and asking questions and trying to model myself after others was worthless. Everything in my ministry was worthless, unless God was in the bush. Only He could make something happen. Only He could make it work.

Thomas told of many Christian workers who failed at first because they thought they had something to offer God. He himself had once imagined that because he was an aggressive, winsome, evangelistic sort, God could use him. But God didn't use him until he came to the end of himself. I thought, *That's exactly my situation. I am at the end of myself.*

When Thomas closed out with Galatians 2:20, it all came together for me:

I have been crucified with Christ; it is no longer I who live, but Christ who lives in me; and the life I now live in the flesh I live by faith in the Son of God, who loved me and gave himself for me (RSV).

I ran back to my room in tears and fell to my knees next to my bunk. I prayed in Spanish, "Lord, now I get it. I understand. I see the light at the end of the tunnel. The whole thing is 'not I, but Christ in me.' It's not what I'm going to do for You but rather what You're going to do through me."

I stayed on my knees until lunchtime, an hour and a half later, skipping my next class to stay in communion with the Lord. I realized the reason I hated myself inside was because I wrongly loved myself outside. I asked God's forgiveness for my pride in thinking I was a step above my countrymen because I had been well-educated and was fluent in English, and because I had spent so much time with Mr. Mereshian and prayed with Keith Bentson and worked in a bank and spoken on the radio and in a tent and in churches, and because I got to come to the United States and mingle with pastors, seminary professors, and other Christian leaders. I had thought I was really something, but God was not active in the bush. I hadn't given Him a chance.

Well, He still had a lot of burning to do, but God was finally in control of this bush. He wanted me to be grateful for all the small hinges He had put in my life, but He didn't want me to place my confidence in those opportunities to make me a better minister or preacher. He wanted me to depend not on myself or my breaks, but on Christ alone—the indwelling, resurrected, almighty Lord Jesus.

I was thrilled to finally realize we have everything we need when we have Jesus Christ literally living in us. Our inner resource is God

Himself, because of our union with Jesus Christ (see Colossians 2:9-15). It's His power that controls our dispositions, enables us to serve, and corrects and directs us (see Philippians 2:13). Out of this understanding comes a godly sense of self-worth.

That day marked the intellectual turning point in my spiritual life. The practical working out of that discovery would be lengthy and painful, but at least the realization had come. It was exciting beyond words. I could relax and rest in Jesus. He was going to do the work through me. What peace there was in knowing I could quit struggling! Theologically, I knew better, but the experience made me feel as if I had just been converted, after trying to serve the Lord on my own for more than eight years.

Too many Christians live the way I lived all those years, because they believe if they pray enough, read enough, study enough, and work enough, they'll be victorious. That's the essence of the flesh, the essence of self. It cannot be done. We cannot work or earn our victories through any self-effort, any more than we could work for our salvation.

I'll never forget the look on the face of an older missionary in Colombia, South America, sometime later, when this truth dawned on him, too.

I'd been asked to speak to a group of missionaries at a conference, during our first year on the mission field after Pat and I were married. My theme was the indwelling Christ as our resource and power to serve.

Afterward, this old missionary gentleman invited me to go for a walk with him. Then, with tears streaming down his face, he told me, "Luis, I have been here on the field for more than forty years. I have worked for God as hard as I could, with every ounce of my being, but it's brought little but frustration. Now I see why.

"Until today, I don't think I have ever really known what it meant to allow the risen Christ to do the living in me. Thank you, brother."

My heart went out to this man, a genuine servant of the Lord, but one who had experienced no victory in his life or ministry. His lack of victory had been evident. It was obvious he had been carrying bitterness and discouragement in his soul, and there hadn't been much fruit in his ministry.

What makes the difference? Perhaps it sounds too easy: rely on the power of the resurrected Christ, rather than on self-control, where the struggle is almost unbearable. Rely on the indwelling power of the Holy Spirit, rather than on grim determination to hang on, which can be like killing yourself.

When temptation comes, turn to God and say, "Lord Jesus, you know that I'm being tempted and that I cannot resist on my own. I'm relying on Your power, and I'm resting in You to turn my thoughts to something else.

"I have the mind of Christ, and therefore, with Your power, I will rely on You to give me the victory. I depend on Your strength and wisdom."

Deciding to get married

My second semester at Multnomah was exciting, although a C in a course studying the New Testament book of Hebrews brought my grade point average down a couple tenths of a point, to a 3.6. Pat could take some of the credit for that. I spent all the time with her that I could. By Valentine's Day, we were unofficially engaged. I didn't exactly ask her to marry me, though.

In my typical romantic fashion, as we walked under an umbrella in the Portland rain, I asked her if she would return to South America with me. She knew what that entailed. And I knew what her "yes" meant, too.

I had been offered the opportunity to apply as a missionary with OC International (the U.S. parent organization of SEPAL) to work in Colombia under Ed Murphy, who was now field director there. That Pat shared my dream was a blessing beyond measure.

Reverend Albert Wollen, pastor of Cedar Mill Bible Church in Portland, rushed Pat and me through his six mandatory premarital counseling sessions. Rev. Wollen had been Pat's pastor since her family had come to Christ when she was a little girl.

Like mine, Pat's parents came to Christ after she was born. Half a century later, while combing through a bookshelf at her parents' house, Pat discovered an unexpected tribute to her spiritual heritage. There she found an old book by D. L. Moody entitled *Wondrous Love*. Pat decided to show it to me, knowing how much I would appreciate a collection of Moody's sermons. On the flyleaf of the book, however, she discovered her grandmother had written these words:

"To Elsie and Willard on Patricia's birth. May her sweet little life be dedicated to Him whose wondrous love never fails. John 3:16, from Mother. June 24, 1937."

A few months before Pat's birth, her grandparents had begun attending a Bible class in downtown Portland. They were boundless in their enthusiasm for their newfound faith in Jesus Christ. Of course they wanted their children and grandchildren to experience that same new life, so they presented Moody's book to Pat's parents.

Pat's parents were less than enthused with the gift. But that didn't stop Pat's grandparents from communicating, by word and by example, the good news of godly living. Within a few short years, both of Pat's parents trusted Christ as Savior, and at the age of eight Pat did, too.

The Gospel messages contained in *Wondrous Love* were preached during Moody's first mission to England. Pat's grandmother never could have guessed that Pat would marry an evangelist who would invest much time preaching the Gospel in England and throughout the world. But the Lord certainly rewarded her desire to impart a godly inheritance to her family.

So, though we were born half a world apart, Pat and I have always been convinced God brought us together. Even before we were married, we somehow knew He had great things ahead for us, as a demonstration of *His* power and glory and grace.

14

A t the end of the school year Pat stayed in Portland and I headed back to Palo Alto to continue my internship with Ray Stedman at Peninsula Bible Church.

It was a long two months for Pat and me. We had utterly no money for phone calls, so all our contact was by mail. In one letter, I confided to Pat that I had received a word from the Lord that thrilled and humbled me.

Now you have to understand that Ray and the other pastors and elders at Peninsula Bible Church simply *didn't* go around making prophecies. And I certainly hadn't told anyone (except Pat) about my dreams for the future. It was still a secret in my heart. After all, I still hadn't even *seen* an evangelistic crusade. Who would take me seriously?

But one day one of the elders, Bob Connell, took me aside and said, "Luis, I believe God's going to use you to win as many souls as Billy Graham—even in this country." I didn't know what to say. But in my heart I felt *God's going to do this*. I knew the day would come.

I had bought Ray's old '55 Buick and, after completing my internship, raced back up the coast. I arrived just a few days before our August 5, 1961 wedding, jointly officiated by Ray Stedman and Pastor Wollen.

Afterward, Pat and I took a two-week honeymoon, eventually driving back down to the San Francisco Bay area, where we were interviewed by the OC International board and accepted for missionary service. Then we hustled back to Portland and packed for our missionary internship in Detroit.

Admittedly, our itinerary right before and after we got married was anything but ideal—and my temper reared its ugly head all too soon.

There are those who say a Christian leader should not use his own failures as examples in his teaching, preaching, and writing. It certainly would be more pleasant to quietly skip over my faults (though I'm not mentioning everything, believe me!). But I don't want anyone to think, because the Lord in His mercy has blessed me in many ways, that I am in any way above the ordinary struggles and battles of life.

I fail. I make mistakes. I struggle with losing my temper and all the other temptations and shortcomings everyone else faces. Absolutely. There are days when I wish that weren't the case. But when I finally found the peace I had searched so long for, I learned that God doesn't take away the temptations or exempt me from failures. He simply assures me He has covered it all (1 John 1:7), and He gives me the power for future victories (2 Timothy 1:7).

Driving to Detroit

Our trip across the country to Detroit was fun. Getting to know each other better was exciting. Pat probably wondered what she had got herself into, when my best-foot-forward courting approach gave way to the real Luis Palau, but she never admits that.

We visited the usual sites people see on their way across the United States, all of them brand-new to me. I was intrigued by Yellowstone National Park and by the Moody Bible Institute, which we saw while spending three nights in a Chicago YMCA with a lot of strange characters. We had no money for anything better.

Along the way, Pat and I talked for hours on end, discovering at one point the two of us held quite different theological views on the sequence of end-time events. For the record, one of us is "premillennial" and the other isn't. Having grown up in both the Anglican and Christian Brethren churches, I wasn't too threatened that Pat didn't see things the way I did. She's just as much a theologian as I am. Besides, as I joke to my friends, Pat will find out I was right all along when Jesus returns in the clouds to take us to heaven. And if she's right, well, it won't be the first time!

Pat and I still very much enjoy discussing theology and other aspects of life. We're both avid readers and thinkers. Her insightful questions, opinions, and comments keep me on my toes, believe me!

Missionary Internship

During our seven months going through the Missionary Internship program in Detroit, I learned a hard but valuable lesson about not controlling my anger, and another about integrating what I'd learned from Major Ian Thomas about the indwelling Christ into every area of life.

The internship program was designed to test whether we could work hand-in-hand with a local church, trust the Lord for our funds, and adapt to any situation. What an understatement.

The church we served worked us hard but neglected us financially (one week the freewill offering we received consisted of twenty-five cents and a few cans of food someone didn't want). And the woman we lived with refused to put a lock on our bedroom door and would burst in at inopportune times. You can imagine how we felt about that! But it built Christian principles into us.

It soon got to be too much for me, and I had thought I could handle just about anything. In my mind, the project was going well beyond the bounds of credibility. Assuming Fred Renich, director of the internship program, knew exactly what was going on, Luis Palau, man of action, blew his stack.

At first, Fred Renich couldn't get a word in as I ranted and raved about the abuses Pat and I were enduring. I finally threatened to leave.

"You don't have to go home," Mr. Renich said. "We're going to rectify the situation and move you next week." But first he addressed my aggressive, explosive personality tendencies. "You have a quiet wife. If you don't learn to put that choleric temperament under the control of Jesus Christ, you're going to walk all over Pat, and she just may not let you know. Then one day you'll have destroyed her, and you won't even realize it."

Walk all over Pat? I was stunned by what Mr. Renich said. I loved Patricia. But Mr. Renich urged me to think back over my life, make a list of all the people I'd hurt along the way, and then do whatever it took to make things right.

The point, I learned, wasn't to try to eradicate my choleric bent, but to bring it under control—God's control. Not long after that, Ray Stedman told me he too was choleric. I could hardly believe it. In my mind, his basic personality was as different from mine as night and day. If a Spirit-controlled choleric could be like Ray Stedman, there was hope for me.

Further mentoring

Fred Renich and I grew very close. I found him to be an excellent teacher and mentor. He helped me learn to apply the principles of the indwelling Spirit to my temperament in all my daily affairs: in marriage, in thinking, in emotions, in service, in preaching, in relationships.

I had tremendous ground to make up, and more than a few old friends and acquaintances to contact so I could apologize for past actions. British writer Rudyard Kipling, of *Jungle Book* fame, and author of many other works, once said, "Nothing is ever settled until it is settled right." I was earnest about settling everything from my past. I didn't want any skeletons that could jump out of the closet and haunt me later in life.

By the summer of 1962, Pat and I were ready to get on with our lives as missionaries. After a brief visit with Pat's family in Portland, we headed to Palo Alto for three weeks of orientation with OC International. While there, we received the shocking news that Pat's mother had contracted polio. She was stricken severely enough that she uses a wheelchair to this day. Elsie Scofield has been an amazing source of inspiration to us, in that she seems to harbor no bitterness. She never complains and is extremely personable . Elsie and Willard are a fantastic couple. Of course, Pat hurried back to be with them for a few weeks before we took off for Fresno, California.

Learning from Billy Graham

Normally after orientation, new missionaries immediately begin their deputation work, raising the support necessary to send them to the field. But since I expected to be heavily involved in evangelistic crusades someday, OC International agreed it would be valuable for us to go to Fresno. There Pat and I helped (strictly as volunteers) with preparations for Billy Graham's July 1962 crusade.

I was so sure evangelism was what I was called to that I was like a hawk in Fresno. I didn't miss a thing. I asked questions of everyone, kept a thick notebook on every detail, and learned the mechanics of mobilizing thousands of people. I tagged along with Bill Brown, the Fresno crusade director, and also visited Spanish churches in the area to urge them to fully cooperate with and participate in the Graham crusade meetings at Ratcliffe Stadium.

Pat worked in special reservations, arranging for the large groups that came by bus and train. During the crusade itself she would work at the counseling table, and I would interpret for the Spanish audience.

At a pre-crusade breakfast we got to meet Billy Graham, and when he discovered my ambition was to preach in evangelistic crusades, he advised staying with the big cities. "Paul always went to the centers of population," he told us. "And Mr. Moody used to say that the cities were the mountains, and if you won the mountains, the valleys took care of themselves."

It was a thrill to have Mr. Graham talk with us, but I wish now we hadn't been too shy to have our pictures taken with him. I've always been a little embarrassed by the line about my being "the new Billy Graham," but if anyone wonders why our team's crusades resemble his in many ways, they should have seen us eagerly absorbing the basics in Fresno. Little did we know at the time we'd be back, twenty-four years later, for a huge citywide crusade of our own.

That same summer Pat and I started our deputation work, with our sights set on working with Ed Murphy in Colombia. I became a full-fledged U.S. citizen. And Pat discovered she was pregnant.

15

The next January, 1963, when Pat was seven months pregnant, she suddenly announced it was time to go to the hospital. I couldn't believe it. We were staying in the home of some friends while doing missionary deputation work at Valley Church in Cupertino, California. I reminded Pat that we were planning to return to Portland before our firstborn arrived on the scene two months later.

Pat said, "Tell that to the baby," and off we went to Stanford University Hospital.

I had been waiting in the hallway for more than an hour when the doctor, a Christian friend from Palo Alto, came and told me there were serious complications.

"What's wrong?"

"I'm not sure yet, Luis. We just have to pray."

I was scared to death. I couldn't sit down as I prayed for Pat and for our baby. I kept trying to peek down the hallway to see where the doctor was. When another hour went by and he hadn't come out again, I feared the worst. When he did come out, he looked more worried than ever. "We're getting an incredibly strong heartbeat for only a seven-month fetus," he said, "and it is so irregular that I must tell you I'm not optimistic. I don't know how the baby is surviving with the heartbeat we're hearing."

Two more hours went by. I kept praying. Finally, I assumed that we had lost the baby. Otherwise, the doctor would have come back. When he finally arrived, he wore a huge grin.

"Congratulations!" he said. "You're the father of twin boys!" What the doctor heard had been *two* regular heartbeats.

Kevin and Keith were premature, less than four pounds each, and had to stay in the hospital for five weeks. I'll never forget the day we finally brought them home. Their chances had been slim for a while and their breathing difficult, but now they're healthy young men.

Language school in Costa Rica

After my ordination at Peninsula Bible Church, our next stop, late that same year, was Costa Rica. We arrived only a few days before Christmas. It was Pat's first time outside the U.S., following on the heels of Kennedy's assassination, and our twins weren't quite a year old.

Knowing what we know now, we shouldn't have tried to leave right when we did, but the Spanish Language Institute where Pat was enrolled began the first of January.

Pat ended up crying her heart out on Christmas Eve. She had so many adjustments to make all at once—moving to a foreign land, far away from family—with the holidays on top of it all.

The good memories we have of that first Christmas are a credit to a super couple, David and Betty Constance, whom we met at language school. They had nearly completed their studies and were preparing to leave for ministry in Argentina, but they came over and we had a fun time together. They continue to be good friends of ours.

After the holidays, we anxiously looked for a housekeeper, something we desperately needed since Pat was going to school. None could be found, so Pat went to school while I stayed home and took care of the twins. Talk about culture shock! Growing up, my sisters Matilde and Martha had always taken care of the younger ones. Latin men simply did not touch babies in those days, except to hug and kiss them. But full-time baby care was my lot for three long weeks.

After a couple of days, I couldn't take it any longer. Impatiently, I told the Lord, "Is this what I came here for? I left my country to go to seminary. I've been through missionary internship. I've completed deputation. I've been ordained. And now here I am on the mission field. But instead of preaching and winning souls, I'm stuck at home, day after day . . . burping babies and changing messy diapers!"

The Lord gently reminded me: "Just a minute, Luis. You are always reminding people that they should trust the Lord and that it is wonderful to have Christ within us in every circumstance. Isn't that right?" It was quite a lesson. Life is a lot of blood, sweat, tears, and dirty little jobs no one else wants to do. The important thing is not what I do, but who I am. Am I willing to be a faithful servant of Christ, no matter what?

First missionary travels

A few weeks later, we had a visit that was a God-send. My mother came up from Argentina to stay with Pat and the twins while I went to Guatemala for five weeks. Mom loved taking care of the grand-children during the day while Pat was in school or at home reviewing her Spanish lessons.

In Guatemala, I preached primarily in Presbyterian churches but also in schools and special meetings. The friends I made there would one day invite me to return for huge evangelistic crusades. In fact, I've spoken more times to more people in Guatemala than anywhere else except Britain.

That five-week ministry tour was an important and fruitful time, but afterward I determined I wouldn't be separated from the whole family for that long a period again, if at all possible.

Some Christian workers feel it's poor stewardship to bring one's spouse or child along on a ministry trip, that it's a waste of money. But is it?

I remember talking to Dr. James Dobson about this. Although I logged millions of miles while my sons were growing up, I probably spent more time with them than the average father. And I cashed in my frequent flier miles, whenever possible, to take them with me when I was speaking at a youth conference or the like. Pat and I ministered together frequently, as well. Instead of getting an hono-rarium, we would ask if we could bring the boys with us when we spoke at family Bible conferences during the summer. We'd do it again in a minute. Those times together were invaluable.

Tensions in Colombia

When we finally arrived in Bogotá, Colombia, in the summer of 1964, I knew OC International expected me to be a regular mission-ary, training nationals in evangelism and church planting. I didn't dare tell anyone I considered this a stepping-stone for a future crusade ministry. The goals of OC fit in perfectly with my dreams of mass evangelism, and the mission has always been biblical and flexible, so I saw little conflict. I needed the experience, so I was willing to start from scratch.

We started with what we called local church mobilization cam-paigns. The idea was to be catalysts to bring churches together across denominational lines and stimulate evangelism. We wanted the man in the pew to learn how to share his faith, lead others to Christ, disciple them, and plant new churches.

We weren't in Bogotá long before we began to feel that city was not the best place for our headquarters. According to all reports, Cali appeared to have a more receptive climate for the Gospel.

Our first effort was with a Christian and Missionary Alliance Church in Cali, where several of us held Colombia's first evangelistic street meetings after a decade of violent persecution and killings. My old friend Bruce Woodman, who was now working at HCJB radio in Quito, Ecuador, came and played the trombone and led singing.

I was glad to have OC field director Ed Murphy behind us because—in the first street meetings especially—the local Christians did not want to get involved. I don't blame them. The situation in Colombia was touchy. For more than a decade, evangelicals had undergone extreme persecution for their faith. Scores had been killed. Preaching in the streets simply was not done. But change was in the air. We were convinced God was going to swing the doors wide open for evangelism in Colombia.

One day, while we were preaching to a small crowd, half a dozen formal religious leaders approached. One of our younger guys met them halfway across the square and defused them by telling them how wonderful it was that local Christians were having a meeting.

"What are they doing?" the six asked.

"They're speaking straight from the Bible."

"Oh, that is good," they agreed. And they went on their way. The current discussions initiated by Pope John XXIII about Protestants simply being separated brethren did us a lot of good in Cali.

So did the intervention of President John Kennedy, before his assassination. During a meeting with evangelist Billy Graham, the president asked why enmity seemed to exist between Catholics and Protestants.

Billy Graham spelled out some of the historical problems and went on to discuss the situation in Colombia at that time. Six months later, Kennedy told Graham that he had done his homework. "You were right on that thing in Colombia. I assure you it's going to stop, and it's going to stop this year."

Radio ministry launched

About that time Bruce Woodman got the idea that I should

occasionally travel to Quito to record a daily evangelistic radio program. Later, we began a daily Bible teaching program, too. Both programs are still broadcast daily on hundreds of radio stations, heard daily by an estimated 22 million people. We receive thousands of letters from listeners every year. Many are won to Christ, and other millions are grounded in their faith. But those early radio years were especially important, helping build the foundation of trust among believers for future crusades and other ministry opportunities all across the Spanish-speaking world.

Our ministry in Colombia continued to be successful, by God's grace. I learned to be used in a variety of ways, but all the while I kept appealing to the home office for more action in evangelistic campaigns.

16

Whenever one of the OC International board members, or the president, Dick Hillis, visited the field, I got him alone and pleaded with him to let me start my own evangelistic team and begin holding evangelistic crusades.

They admitted they had started me small so I could learn many things, including humility, but they weren't ready to turn me loose for mass crusades just yet. Santiago Garabaya was considered the better evangelist, and I the Bible teacher on OC's Colombia staff. That may have been accurate, but I felt an evangelist should also be a solid Bible teacher, so it certainly shouldn't have been considered a liability.

I was now in my thirties and felt as if opportunities in mass evangelism were passing me by. I had learned a lot and had big dreams, but I couldn't do it on my own. It seemed logical to me that OC should allow such a crusade team within the mission, but they weren't sure I was ready for it yet. And they were probably right. At least my wife, Pat, thought so!

First church campaign

The first local church campaign I remember I was allowed to do on my own was at La Floresta Presbyterian Church in Cali, in September of 1965. I knew if our strategy was going to work in big citywide crusades, it would have to work in small local churches, too. La Floresta qualified as just that. The church had about sixty members.

My goal was to spend the first week addressing the spiritual condition of the people in the church. There's no point mobilizing Christians for evangelism and discipleship if they haven't confessed known sin, experienced God's forgiveness, consecrated their lives to the Lord, and begun to enjoy the Christ-centered, Spirit-filled life.

The plan was precise and theologically sound, and eventually we got it all in. But I nearly didn't get past the second night. Revival broke out! After a dramatic, divine breakthrough, people got right with God, and by the end of two weeks we saw more than one hundred twenty-five people trust Christ as Savior. About eighty joined that congregation. The church was in a state of revival for months on end, overflowing with spontaneous evangelism and joy. The minister, John Lovelace, an outstanding missionary, and I became fast friends and prayer partners over the years.

I could hardly sleep during those two weeks. Several of us walked around town at night, too excited to sleep, praying, and dreaming big dreams for the future. If God can do this in one local church, what else can He do?

Television ministry launched

Two months later, we flew back to Quito to test a new concept— live counseling television broadcasts—that would reach vast numbers for Christ. We started with a short program, but people kept calling in even after we went off the air. So we kept the program on the air, longer and longer. After a couple of weeks, we were staying on the air three hours at a time.

It was exhausting, but invigorating. The Lord had given me the ability to think quickly under pressure, but this program required rapid recall of many specific Scriptures. It was good I had enjoyed studying the Bible, but now I was forced to go at it with a vengeance, storing up God's answers for the myriad of problems represented by callers from all walks of life.

It seemed the phones didn't stop ringing, once we went on the air. I never knew what to expect. One person on the verge of suicide would call in. The next person would be going through a messy divorce.

One night I received two consecutive calls, the first of which was one of the most rewarding ever on the program. The other turned into one of the most bizarre encounters in our entire ministry.

The first caller was a young airline stewardess who had seen her parents' marriage break up. She decided if her father—a judge on the high court—could live in sin, so could she. And so she did. She was having an affair with a young Colombian doctor. She was miserable, repentant, and desperate to be forgiven.

It had not been my practice to lead callers to Christ on the air. Instead, I would counsel them from the Scriptures and set up in-person appointments where I could carefully show them the way of salvation at the studio counseling office the next day.

But this woman was desperate. When I read to her from the Bible that God loved her and offered her forgiveness and salvation, she wanted to receive Him right then and there. I hesitated. Did I want to do this on the air? Would it look like a setup? Was it a good precedent? It was obvious she was sincere.

I asked her to pray with me and added that anyone else watching by television who wanted to pray along with us and receive Christ could do so. "Dear God," I began, "I know I am a sinner." She repeated each line. "I have broken a sacred marriage. I have done a hateful thing to a man's wife and children." And we prayed on, recounting the sins she had told me. "Father, I need Your forgiveness and Your saving love." It was a tearful, solemn, anointed moment as she prayed to receive Christ.

Moments like that are some of the most effective and emotion-filled of all my ministry. Potentially hundreds of thousands of people are listening in, and who knows how many come to Christ each time?

The young stewardess was so excited that she insisted upon an appointment the next morning at nine.

The next caller was brief. A tiny, high-pitched, squeaky voice simply requested an appointment the next day at nine-thirty. No more conversation. When I agreed, the squeaky voice simply thanked me and hung up.

Maria's story

The next morning, after I had counseled the young stewardess and encouraged her in her new-found faith, I walked her to the door. I was giving her a Bible and some literature when I noticed a little woman walking through the gates of the HCJB property, followed closely by two huge, able-bodied men who could have passed for American football players.

As she entered the office, I asked if the two gentlemen would like to come in, too. "No," she said, "one will stand by the door and the other by the gate." It was the squeaky voice from the night before, and she was right on time.

She brushed past me and felt along the bottom edges of the desk top, as if looking for something. Without explanation, she moved to the wall and peeked behind a hanging picture. Her eyes traveled to every corner before she finally sat down. I thought she must be unbalanced.

She swore and smoked quite unlike anyone I had ever met before. She attacked each cigarette, sucking every last bit from it and then lit the next with the smoldering butt of the last.

In spite of her tiny voice, she spoke through a sneer, and venom poured out. Her voice dripped with sarcasm and hatred. "You pastors and priests," she began with disgust. "You are a bunch of thieves and liars and crooks. All you want is to deceive people; all you want is money!"

She went on that way for more than twenty minutes, swearing constantly, and accusing, criticizing, and insulting. Bitterness gushed from her and left me speechless. I had no idea how to react and couldn't have got a word in, anyway. I prayed silently, *Lord, how shall I handle this?*

Seemingly exhausted from the ordeal, she finally slumped in her chair like a jogger who just has finished a tough course. She took a deep breath, her eyes still flashing.

"Madam," I began, "is there anything I can do for you? How can I help you?"

She slowly took her cigarette from her lips and sat staring at me for an instant, then suddenly broke into uncontrollable sobs. I continued to pray silently, *Lord, what am I going to do? I'm no psychiatrist. I'm just a preacher. Why did You send her to me? She seems insane.*

When she was composed and could speak again, the edge was gone from her voice. "You know," she said, "in the thirty-eight years I have lived, you are the first person who has ever asked me if he could help me. All my life people have come to me with their hands out, saying, 'Help me, come here, do this, go there, do that.'"

"What is your name?" I asked.

She was suddenly hard again. "Why do you want to know my name?"

"Well, you've said a lot of things here, and I don't even know you. I just want to know how to address you."

She sat back in her chair and straightened up a bit. Cocking her head and looking at me out of the corner of her eye, she lifted her chin and took yet another drag at her cigarette. Then she said with finality, "I'm going to tell you," as if allowing me a real privilege.

Luis Palau

"My name is Maria," she said triumphantly. I recognized her last name as that of a large family of wealth and influence. "I am the secretary of the Communist Party here in Ecuador. I am a Marxist-Leninist, and I am a materialist. I don't believe in God."

With that she took off on another breathless tirade against all preachers and priests, the church, the Bible, and anything else she could think of that rivaled her beliefs.

"Why did you come here?" I broke in. "Just to insult me, or what?"

She was thoughtful again. "I'm going to tell you my story," she announced. And for the next three hours, without pause or interruption, she did just that.

She had been a rebellious teenager who ran away from a religious school and was given a choice by her parents: return to school or leave the family. She left. The communists befriended her and took her in. Within the next few years, she married and divorced three times and had several children.

Despite her upbringing, she became a party leader and organized student rebellions. Her story was like the plot of a grade-B movie. I let her talk on and on, wondering when her first sign of vulnerability would surface.

17

Maria continued to tell her story in machine-gun fashion, interrupting her narrative only occasionally to emphatically remind me of her list of titles and beliefs and nonbeliefs. She made it quite clear that, as a Marxist-Leninist, she opposed everything that Christianity stood for.

I kept praying, *When will the opening come?* Three hours after she began, we finally got down to business.

"Listen, Palau," Maria said. "Supposing there is a God—and I'm not saying there is, because I don't believe in the Bible, and I don't believe there's a God—but just supposing there is. Just for the sake of chatting about it, if there is a God—which there isn't—do you think He would receive a woman like me?"

So this poor, frightened, little woman with the big facade had a chink in her armor, after all! Years before, studying Dr. R. A. Torrey's book *How to Work for Christ*, I had learned that when dealing with a professed atheist, the best approach is to take one verse from the Bible and stay with it, driving it home until it sticks, repeating it as many times as necessary. The Bible says that the law of the Lord converts the soul, not the arguments of men.

Which verse suits her? I wondered. The Lord gave me Hebrews 10:17, one of my favorites, because it is so short and says so much: "'Their sins and their lawless deeds I will remember no more'" (NKJV).

I said, "Look, Maria, don't worry about what I think; look at what God thinks." I opened to the verse and turned the Bible so she could see it.

"But I don't believe in the Bi. . . . "

"You've already told me that," I said. "But we're just supposing there's a God, right? Let's just suppose this is His Word. He says, 'Their sins and their lawless deeds I will remember no more.'"

She waited, as if there had to be more. I said nothing. "But, listen.

I've been an adulteress, married three times, and in bed with a lot of different men."

I said, "'Their sins and their lawless deeds I will remember no more,'" and began to count the times I repeated it.

"But I haven't told you half my story. I stabbed a comrade who later committed suicide."

"'Their sins and their lawless deeds I will remember no more.'"

"I've led student riots where people were killed!"

"'Their sins and their lawless deeds I will remember no more.'"

"I egged on my friends and then hid while they were out dying for the cause."

"'Their sins and their lawless deeds I will remember no more.'"

Seventeen times I responded to Maria's objections and confessions with that one Bible verse. It was past lunchtime. I was tired and weak. I had no more to offer. "Would you like Christ to forgive all that you've told me about, and all the rest that I don't even know?"

She was quiet. Finally she spoke softly. "If He could forgive me and change me, it would be the greatest miracle in the world." I led her in a simple prayer of commitment. By the end, she was crying.

Maria returned, a week later, to tell me that she was reading the Bible and that she felt a lot better. A longtime missionary from HCJB agreed to follow her up, but I was not prepared for what I would encounter when I saw Maria again, two months later.

Vicious persecution

In January 1966, a month before our son Andrew's birth, we went back to Quito for more television counseling and radio-program taping. While there, we were again visited by our favorite little revolutionary. I was shocked. Her face was a mess of purple blotches and bruises. Several front teeth were missing.

Shortly after I had last seen her, Maria told her comrades about her new faith. At a meeting of all the communist leaders of the country, she told them, "I am no longer an atheist. I believe in God and in Jesus Christ, and I have become a Christian. I am resigning from the party, and I don't want to have anything more to do with it. We are all a bunch of liars. We deceive people when we tell them there is no God.

"Of course there is a God! Look at the garden outside. Do you think the flowers created themselves? Are you going to tell me everything is the result of some explosion in space billions of years ago?"

It was as if Maria had let a bunch of hungry lions out of a cage. The leaders fought among themselves, some trying to shout her down and get at her, another insisting that she should be allowed to speak.

A few days later she was nearly run down by a Jeep full of her former comrades. The next day several of her former protégés—militant university students—attacked her and smashed her face against a utility pole until she was unconscious.

Maria was forced to hide out in the basements of several churches and in the homes of missionaries, always on the run. For her and the HCJB missionary to be able to study the Bible, they first had to drive around until they were sure no one was following them.

I was amazed at the persecution she had suffered as such a young believer. "There's going to be a revolution in June," she told me matter-of-factly. "We've had it all planned for months."

It was to be a typical Latin American uprising: students and agitators causing a disturbance in the streets, luring out the army, which would then be attacked and if possible overthrown. The military junta then would be forced to leave the country, and the chairman of the Communist Party for Ecuador would come out of hiding in Colombia and take over the country.

Maria remained on the run until June. On the morning of the revolution, the Communist Party leader came out of Colombia to talk to Maria. In a few hours he was to become the new ruler of the country, but first he wanted to talk to his longtime friend.

"Maria," he asked, "why did you become a Christian?"

"Because I believe in God and in Jesus Christ, and my faith has changed my life."

"You know," he said, "while hiding out, I have been listening to HCJB radio on shortwave, and those—they almost have *me* believing there is a God!"

"There is!" she said. "Why don't you become a Christian and get out of this business? We never had any real convictions about atheism and materialism. And look at all the lives we've ruined and all the terrible things we've been into. Here, take this Bible and this book [*Peace with God*, by Billy Graham]. You can go to my father's farm and read them."

Miraculously, he accepted her offer. Later that morning, the disturbance that was supposed to trigger a revolution fizzled into chaos, and Ecuador was saved from anarchy, tyranny, and worse.

Of the many, many people I have seen come to Christ over the years, Maria has one of the wildest stories. But when I saw the effect of her conversion on the history of an entire country, it solidified in me a burden, not just for individuals, but also for nations.

Promoting positive social change

Back in Cali, several of my OC colleagues joined me for a late night rendezvous on the twenty-fifth floor of a downtown hotel. From the hotel's roof-top restaurant, we looked out over the city center. The boulevards stretched in all directions, the lush green metropolis teemed with hundreds of thousands of people who had never heard the Gospel. Long past midnight we planned and dreamed.

How can we reach this city for Christ? we pondered as we looked out over the city "with the eyes of God." How such an exercise tears the heart. How the prayers of the Holy Spirit pour out!

In subsequent days, we took long walks through the hot and humid city streets, passing middle- and upper-class houses with spacious lawns protected by guard dogs and high walls, wondering how to break through their indifference to the claims of Christ.

We walked through the slums, our hearts broken and almost weeping at what we saw. We already were spending the little money we had to help churches and local Christian groups set up cooperatives to help the poorest of the poor. But we dreamed of the day we would see the Gospel revolutionize the masses, lifting them from their poverty and vices by the power of God's Holy Spirit.

In hundreds of press conferences and university speeches since then, I have gone on record saying Latin America has all the resources to enjoy a successful standard of living, but it has been undermined by rampant immorality and a lack of ethics. I saw it growing up in Argentina. I saw it there in Cali, Colombia. Even United Nations research has documented that more than seven out of every ten Latin children are born out of wedlock. The average Latin man between the ages of 35 and 45 has had children by at least three women. For all his *machismo*, his income would instantly double if only he gave up gambling, drinking, and other vices.

"Such blatant disregard for biblical principles destroys homes, wrecks the economy, and weakens nations," I've told thousands of

Latin American journalists and university professors. Nobody has ever challenged me.

Who can dispute the direct relationship between a nation's moral values and behavior and the overall well-being of that nation?

Lately, I've been tempted to make this same point as I hold press conferences and speak in universities across America. I love this country. I'm not an American by accident; I chose to become an American. I'm proud of this nation.

But we have to realize we're enjoying the tail end of the blessings of the past. We still think we're a superior nation, not realizing the glory is departing. We're almost as bad off now as Latin America was in the 1960s. The only difference is countries like Colombia and Guatemala are on the way up and America is passing them on the way down. As a nation, we need to honor the Lord once again and change direction—fast!—before God abandons us to judgment.

Right before leaving on furlough in December 1966, Pat and I received a wonderful answer to prayer and saw Colombia's first national spiritual breakthrough. It would prove to be a glorious finale to our first term as missionary-evangelists.

18

U ndoubtedly, my impatience and eagerness to turn a corner and get into some true citywide crusade evangelism was hard on Ed Murphy and the whole OC staff. It's a good thing they liked me and saw that I was truly committed to Christ and to sharing His love.

It was all they could do to put up with my constant reminders that "Life is going by too fast. I want to redeem the time. I'm more than thirty years old!" I later learned that one OC leader returned from the mission field and told the board of directors, "We may have to clip Luis' wings."

I was getting desperate to get moving, figuring it would take several years to expand beyond local church campaigns to united citywide evangelistic crusades. If I let the years slip by, I'd be an old man, still hoping and dreaming foolish dreams. I didn't want that to happen, and I was ready to move out on my own, if necessary.

When Ray Stedman was in Guatemala for a pastors' conference, he flew me over to see him. "Be patient," was his advice. That was like telling an amputee not to cry.

"How long must I sit around and sit around?" I wanted to know. "If I have to leave OC and start on my own from scratch, I may do it."

"Be patient," he repeated. "If God is in it, it will happen when the time is right."

Just before attending the World Congress on Evangelism in Berlin, late in 1966, I began receiving correspondence from OC board member Vic Whetzel about considering Mexico as a fertile ground for mass evangelism. I had never considered it before, but I gave it some thought. I wasn't sure what he was driving at. Would Pat and I be asked to switch mission fields?

Berlin summit

I found the setting for the World Congress on Evangelism almost as fascinating as the plenary sessions and workshops themselves. Back in Colombia and other parts of Latin America, communists were fervently trying to win the day. Standing at the edge of West Berlin, I shuddered as I thought of the oppression millions were enduring such a short distance away to the east. On the Berlin Wall I read these words in large letters: "How long will this go on?"

One dark, cold afternoon, when the congress meetings had let out early and many of the 1,200 delegates were milling around West Berlin, I received a call from OC board members Dr. Ray Benson and Dr. Dick Hillis. They wanted to take a walk with me and have a chat. We walked for a long time before they got to their point.

"Luis," Dick said, "we feel you and Pat should go home on furlough in December as planned. Once your furlough is over, begin to develop your own evangelistic team with your sights set on Mexico. You'll be field director for Mexico, with your headquarters there."

For once I was speechless. A dream had come true. I am grateful to OC for patiently working with me. Who knows what would have happened to me or my ministry if they had let me go off on my own when I was making all that noise.

I had no connections or contacts in the States, outside of my few friends on the West Coast. My major concern was whether I could have OC team member Joe Lathrop on my team. Dick and Ray agreed readily and asked what else they could do for me. I knew we would need a music man, too, and we arranged for Bruce Woodman to work with us.

Dick Hillis told me he hoped I would "become the greatest evangelist in the world." Coming from a man who was prayerfully concerned about any potential ego problems, that was a comment I knew exactly how to take. It reflected his attitude. He wanted nothing for my glory, everything for God's glory. So did I. What a father in Christ Dr. Hillis has been to me, together with Norm Cummings, OC's home director for many years.

First citywide crusade

Just before leaving Colombia for Argentina—where my new family would celebrate Christmas with my original family before returning to the United States for our furlough—it was time to keep a promise I had made to a band of Christian young people who wanted to make an impact on Bogotá.

Ed Murphy and I had met with little success in Bogotá before setting up shop in Cali, so this was an exciting proposition for us. The national organization of Christian young people had scheduled a parade and a four-day crusade in Bogotá, December 8-12, 1966. "Even if we get killed, come what may, we'll do it," they told me, "if you'll help us." They knew the rally could shake up their country and open it once and for all to the Gospel.

Several months earlier, I had advised these young people to set high sights for Colombia, to plan a presidential prayer banquet, and to seek to have a born-again Christian elected president someday. Eleven years later, many of us were reunited at the elegant Tequindama Hotel in Bogotá following the first presidential prayer banquet in Colombia's history. They had waited a long time for that answer to prayer, and it was an emotional time, believe me! Even *Time* magazine covered the event, reporting that 2,500 civic leaders (including four presidential candidates and various military leaders) attended the "Banquet of Hope":

> The principal guest, Colombia's President Alfonso Lopez Michelsen, showered Palau with congratulations. He responded with a blunt plea for the Colombian elite to turn to God and foster a spiritual reawakening. The Colombians who arranged the banquet, Palau told *TIME*, think that "the only ideology that can stop Marxist-Leninism or the disintegration of our society is Evangelical Christianity."

When I arrived in Bogotá to work with the youth leaders in early December 1966, I was amazed at what had been done already. Thousands of Christians in surrounding towns had been invited to converge in the capital city, December 8.

The parade was going to be a huge one. We allowed no more than four people in a row and spread them out so they stretched twelve city blocks.

Everyone was instructed to hold his Bible over his heart. The gesture was pregnant with symbolism. The young people were not just expressing how highly they esteemed the Bible. They also were saying: "I dare you to come and kill me."

As well, everyone was instructed to carry a small transistor radio. We had purchased radio time from one of the local stations so we could broadcast a selection of Christian songs during the march. With everyone tuned into the music on that station, it was a simple but brilliant way to synchronize the singing all the way down the line as 7,000 young people marched from the Intercontinental Hotel down Seventh Avenue to Bolivar Plaza, a huge square bordered by government offices and the main cathedral.

It was impressive, but dangerous. To be honest, I was frightened. Anything could have happened. The stonings and killings could have begun again. We had asked the police to close some streets to traffic, but no answer had been given. Shortly after the parade got under way, we saw red lights flashing. Police cars were coming. Many in the march froze. So this would be it.

What happened next surprised us all. When the police cars reached the front of the parade, they took positions leading the march, red lights still flashing, helping clear the avenue for us.

The somber atmosphere became one of joy when the thousands of young people realized the parade was a great success. The singing grew louder, the smiles broader, the steps lighter. Posters and banners with Bible verses swung in the air with more enthusiasm than ever.

As the columns marched forward, many older Christians (including a group of missionaries and national pastors) who had been looking on from a safe distance joined in. Others did the same, including half a dozen priests and a group of nuns.

The crowds continued to swell. Twelve thousand people followed the parade (the next day's newspaper said 30,000) to Bolivar Plaza, where, we heard later, the archbishop peeked out his cathedral window to see what was happening.

The president even came out of his office and asked what was going on, then commented to one of the youth leaders, "If you can draw a crowd like this, you could get a president elected." (So, our dream wasn't all that wild, after all. Even the president agreed!)

By the time I was ready to speak, 20,000 people had jammed the plaza. I was beside myself. Standing on the stairway of the main government building, I preached on "Christ the Liberator" (John 8:36).

At the end of the brief message, three hundred people raised their hands, publicly committing their lives to Jesus Christ, and several hundred more were saved during the crusade meetings over the next four nights.

It was an historic moment for Colombia and indeed for all of Latin

America. Never before had people committed to Christ made such a dramatic impact. It was obvious that a new era had begun.

What a way to end one missionary term and start looking forward to the next!

No longer would I have to fret, wondering about and waiting for my chance to get into crusade evangelism on a larger scale. By God's grace, we were on our way! On furlough we spread the word everywhere that Bruce and Joe and I were a new team and ready to share Christ's message with all of Mexico.

Ministry objectives

During a missions conference in the Pacific Northwest, I drafted a memo to the board of OC on the goals, objectives, and strategies of the Luis Palau Evangelistic Association. That memo became the foundation paper for our work. Over the years, our team has grown by leaps and bounds. We've added executives, crusade directors, administrative assistants, media specialists, accountants, and other necessary staff. We now have more than 60 staff members working out of our headquarters and regional offices around the world.

But it's surprising how little our overall team philosophy has changed. In dependence upon God, our objectives still are:

- to win as many people as possible to Jesus Christ throughout the world, proclaiming His Good News by all available means to the millions of people who have yet to respond to the Gospel.

- to emphasize with the church the principles of victorious Christian living (Galatians 2:20), so as to stimulate, revive, train, and mobilize the Church to continuous, effective evangelism, follow-up, and church growth.

- to hold high the banner of biblical evangelism, influencing Christianity worldwide and raising up a new generation of godly leaders, so that the Church's commitment to evangelism will never die.

19

For almost a year and a half we were on furlough and doing deputation work. Besides visiting Pat's family, highlights included speaking at two missions conferences.

During the missions conference at Multnomah Bible College and Biblical Seminary, held at the nearby Central Bible Church, I arrived late for a Friday morning session. At the entrance of the church I saw Dr. Ted Bradley, president of the seminary and my former professor of Biblical Anthropology. I was surprised he wasn't in the session, so I walked up and asked, "Dr. Bradley, how are you? You look a little tired."

Quietly, Dr. Bradley said, "Yes."

"Was the work organizing the conference this week pretty hard on you?"

Again, in a weak voice, he said, "Yes." Then he explained: "The thing that is dragging me down a little is the fact that Virginia [his second daughter] left yesterday for Nigeria. Luis, we're so happy, but it is awfully hard to see her go." I had seen Virginia the previous Saturday, a tiny little thing. She and another single young woman were going out with Wycliffe Bible Translators to work with a tribe in some isolated corner of Africa

After mentioning Virginia's departure, Dr. Bradley started to weep. He was happy and sad, at the same time. "You know, Luis, she was so little, so frail, it just hurts to see her go so alone. I'm afraid I'll never see her again." As it turns out, he didn't. Dr. Bradley went to be with the Lord before his daughter's first furlough.

Evangelism is social action

Three weeks later, while in Palo Alto to speak at Peninsula Bible Church's annual missions conference, I had lunch with several men from Stanford University. As I talked about the results we'd seen in Colombia and our dreams for Mexico, one professor looked me square in the eye and asked, point blank: "Palau, how can you go to country after country, where people have such vast economic and social problems, and preach about the resurrected Christ? Can't you do something more practical for them?" It wasn't the first time I'd been asked that question, and certainly not the last.

"There isn't a better way to help them," I replied. "The people of this world create the problems of this world. If we can lead them to Christ, we will create a climate for other positive, practical changes to take place."

The question came up again during a recent radio program. I told the interviewer and his listening audience I'm all for social activism: "Go ahead and do it, it's a good thing to do. But if you want to see people turned around, they've got to have Christ in their hearts—He is the only One who can change lives."

Moving to Mexico City

We finally arrived in Mexico in mid-1968, eager to share Christ with the nation. We had high hopes. After testing the waters with a local church campaign in Mexico City, I flew back to Colombia for back-to-back crusades in three of the largest cities. During the last one, in Medellín, the local crusade committee came to me and said, "This is going so well, let's have another week of meetings."

I didn't have the guts to tell them I wanted to go back to Mexico. I missed Pat and the boys, true. But it also just so happened that Mexico City was hosting the 1968 Summer Olympics, and I had free tickets for several great events that next week. It was a once-in-a-lifetime opportunity I'd have to miss. Why? The apostle Paul explains it best:

> Do you not know that in a race all the runners run, but only one gets the prize? Run in such a way as to get the prize. Everyone who competes in the [Olympic] games goes into strict training. They do it to get a crown that will not last; but we do it to get a crown that will last forever (1 Corinthians 9:24-25).

That first year in Mexico was particularly rough on Pat. Costa Rica had been tough, Colombia tougher still. And now I'd taken her to Mexico, where she had to start all over learning another culture and another distinct way of speaking Spanish. Besides, she had her hands full with three growing boys and another soon on the way. And, because of a colossal transportation snafu, we had to go without furniture for months on end. It was more than any woman should have to bear.

At one point, I called my mother-in-law and encouraged her to invite Pat and the kids to Portland for four to six weeks. I said I would finance it, but that Pat must not know it was my idea.

Crusade ministry launched

With the help of Joe Lathrop and a new OC man, John McWilliam, we staged fourteen campaigns in Mexico in 1969 alone. The big one was in a bullring in Monterrey, where more than 30,000 heard the Gospel in nine days, and 2,000 made decisions for Christ—including Jose, the printer who produced the crusade advertising.

There in Monterrey a young pastor, fresh out of Bible college, totally immersed his tiny congregation in the crusade. The church was in a rough "drugs-and-muggings" neighborhood. They brought drug addicts, prostitutes, everyone they could to the meetings. By the end of the crusade, fifteen new families were added to the church. One drug addict who was converted through the witness of that church later became pastor of a church in a nearby city.

Although our work of crusade evangelism was finally launched, and God was blessing the work with thousands of conversions, those days were some of the roughest in our ministry. Money was low, and we had to wait and hope and pray that it would come in. You can learn many spiritual lessons from that experience, but you also can find your family living at an impractical level and wondering why.

A gigantic crusade we planned for and promoted at a baseball park in Mexico City was canceled at the last minute by the government. This was more than two decades before President Carlos Salinas de Gortari proposed a series of changes to the nation's constitution that swept away seventy-five years of tight religious restrictions.

We were discouraged—all of us. I wondered if we would ever get on our feet. We vowed to have that big crusade in Mexico City, somehow, someway.

With the baseball park off limits, we scheduled crusade meetings in two of the oldest and most respected Protestant churches in Mexico City that happen to stand back-to-back. By staggering meeting times, I was able to close the first meeting, dash out the back door, and rush to the second in time to start preaching again. It was a gruelling schedule, reminiscent of something D. L. Moody had tried (and quickly tired of!) a century earlier. But given the circumstances we had found ourselves in, it worked. Over the course of fifteen days we saw more than 2,000 people make public commitments to Christ.

Changed lives

People sometimes ask me, "Luis, is it worth it? Does the fruit last?" Does it! Twenty years after those rather impromptu simultaneous crusades in the heart of Mexico City, I met one of the decision-makers in Guatemala City. Not only is he going on for the Lord, he's now a full-time Wycliffe missionary completing the translation of the New Testament into a northern Guatemalan language.

Another decision-maker had been a night club singer in Mexico City. She was soundly converted, joined a local church, grew in her new-found faith, and five years later served as a soloist at our Netzahualcoyotl crusade just east of Mexico City.

A third decision-maker had been a rabid Marxist-Leninist university student. He met a quiet, sweet fellow university student. He was attracted to her and started spending all the free time he could with her.

One day she said, "Carlos, come with me to a youth meeting."

"What's it about?"

"Youth and sex."

"Let's go!"

Until the meeting began, he didn't realize it was one of our crusade youth nights. He almost stomped out when the choruses were sung. Religious stuff! But sex intrigued him so he stayed. The viewpoint of the Bible gripped his mind, and in one sweeping strike the Holy Spirit swept him that very hour into the kingdom of God. What a change! "Instant salvation," as Moody used to call it.

What happened to Carlos? Ask the Campus Crusade for Christ staff in Mexico. He instantly rejected communism, joined a local church, was baptized, took the discipleship training Campus Crusade had to offer, and led more than 120 other people to Christ while working on his psychology degree.

"Does the fruit last?" Thousands of decision-makers I've met again later on or heard from over the years would emphatically say "yes!"

That November, our fourth son, Stephen, was born, adding a nice touch to a difficult year. Good thing Pat and I both love boys!

The next year, 1970, we had a long, exhausting but very fruitful crusade in El Salvador's capital. As if a full schedule every day wasn't enough, I had to race from the stadium to the studios of Channel 4 in San Salvador every night for our live television counseling program.

Back at the hotel one night, Bruce Woodman and I had just gone to our separate rooms when the phone rang. The desk clerk said someone in the lobby was anxious to talk with me. It was 1:45 a.m. My first thought was, *I've been up since 7:00 yesterday morning, and now some drunk wants to talk!*

I called Bruce and we went down to the lobby to find a rather distinguished looking gentleman waiting for us. He was visibly shaking. "I watched your program three hours ago," he said, "and it hit home to my problem. I began to weep and my teenage daughter said, 'Dad, why don't you go and talk to him? He might be able to help you with your drinking problem.'"

Not only did he have a drinking problem, he also confessed he was persistently unfaithful to his wife, even though he was a well-known psychologist who counseled others. "I can't control myself. I'm living like a dog!" He pounded his fist on the coffee table, then pleaded: "Is there any hope of change for a hypocrite like me?"

20

Several people had strolled out of the hotel bar and were in the lobby watching from a distance. Bruce and I presented Christ in His almighty power to our less-than-sober psychologist friend. I've seldom dealt with such an earnest man. Finally he said, "I want to receive Christ right now." He got on his knees in the middle of the lobby, where we led him in prayer.

A week later, during our final live television broadcast, the very last phone call went like this: "Mr. Palau, do you remember the man you talked to at 3:00 in the morning in the hotel? That's me."

I had to ask, "Have you experienced any change this past week?"

"A complete change! And now my wife is here to talk to you." Remember, we were on the air and the conversation was broadcast nationwide.

"Have you seen a change in your husband this past week?"

Not only had she, but she wanted to receive Christ, too! Once again, on the air, we sensed the miracle of regeneration taking place—before an estimated audience of 450,000. (On any given night those two weeks, we had no less than 66 percent of the national viewing audience, according to an independent polling agency hired by the station owner.)

1970 Mexico City crusade

Back in Mexico, getting on television was still only a distant dream. Even holding large-scale crusades seemed next to impossible. Then we heard that another religious group had drawn a big crowd to a convention, so we called our next Mexico City crusade a convention, too, advertising only over our radio programs and by word-of-mouth. We didn't want the authorities to shut us down again.

The response was overwhelming. The crusade drew more than 106,000 people in ten days. Nearly 6,675 people committed their lives to Christ. Churches doubled in size almost overnight. It was the greatest response to the Gospel we'd ever seen. We were ecstatic!

In many ways, that 1970 crusade was the catalyst that began to focus the attention of many on what God was doing. Crusade evangelism was finally on the map south of the border. One journalist reporting on the crusade's impact called me "the Billy Graham of Latin America." Others picked up the story, and the word started getting around.

Slowly but surely, our dream was becoming a reality. The stadiums were now opening up to us. The media were too. Years of hard work and perseverance were starting to pay off. We were reaching the masses!

Expanding the ministry team

That same year Jim Williams—another new OC missionary and a graduate of Biola College and Talbot Theological Seminary—joined our team. At first I was upset because I felt he was sent without my getting a chance to interview him, let alone get to know him. I fired off a letter to OC, asking why they sent a man with whom I was unfamiliar. Then when he arrived he seemed so quiet and hadn't yet learned Spanish fluently.

Jim soon mastered Spanish, however, and became an expert in biblical counseling. He also proved to be a theologian par excellence. He has been with me ever since and is vice president of our Latin American ministries, overseeing our extensive Spanish crusade, radio, television, video, counseling, training courses, conferences, seminars, and publishing ministries. In the latter capacity, he serves as editor-in-chief of our monumental *Continente Nuevo* Bible commentary series and quarterly magazine for pastors.

During that period we added other key people, an individual at a time, from Guatemala, Ecuador, and other nations, developing the first truly international, interdenominational evangelistic team in Latin American history.

Apologies

On one visit to OC headquarters in California, I called ahead and asked if Ed Murphy would meet me at the airport. The request sounded a bit unusual, but I had my reasons. In the car, I told Ed, "I asked for you to meet me because I want to apologize, Ed, for treating you unfairly when I was a missionary in Colombia."

He later admitted he almost fainted. He tried to apologize for some of the difficulties we had had. But I said, "No, I'm a director now, and I have a team full of young, headstrong men. I don't know how you ever put up with me. I was selfish and critical of you. Will you forgive me?" Later I apologized publicly at OC headquarters during the international strategy meetings we were having.

Back home, there were other, more difficult apologies to make. I sensed there was something between me and one of my twins, Keith. So I talked with him and asked, "Keith, have I done anything that really hurt your feelings?"

Instantly, Keith said, "Yes. Last Christmas you promised to buy me a toy and you never gave it to me."

The fact is, I'd completely forgotten about it. I probed further: "Is there anything else I've done that wasn't right and I've never asked for your forgiveness?"

Again, instantly, Keith said, "Yes."

"And what was that?"

"Remember when Mom said you had to go to the hospital because Stephen was going to be born? You left us at home and took off in a hurry. Remember?" I did.

"Well, you took off, you left Mom at the hospital, and you forgot the suitcase with all the stuff." I couldn't believe all the details he remembered! "So you came back and you were real huffy. When you got here, the suitcase had been opened and everything was thrown all over the place. And you spanked me." My heart sank.

"And you didn't do it?" I asked.

"No, I didn't." I felt terrible. I hugged Keith and asked him to forgive me. There was an instant improvement in our relationship after that.

That went so well that I called in Keith's twin brother, Kevin. After all, maybe I'd hurt him, too. "Have I ever done something wrong and never asked your forgiveness or promised you something and never fulfilled my promise?" I asked.

Without any hesitation, Kevin said, "Yes."

"What was it?"

"Last Christmas you promised us a toy and you never bought it for us." Kevin had no idea I'd just talked to Keith about the same thing. Naturally, I took my sons to the store that day and bought them what I'd promised. The important thing wasn't the toy, all the rage at the time. It was a big deal to my boys, obviously. The problem was I'd made a promise all too lightly, dropping the ball (once again) as their father.

On many occasions, before leaving on a ministry trip, I would feel, *Lord, it just isn't worth leaving my family, unless some souls are saved.* To be gone so much of the time from Pat and the boys never was easy. Coming back home knowing I sometimes had to turn around and leave again in a few days was even harder. At times, trying to fulfill all my obligations as a husband and father and an evangelist seemed impossible. The only way Pat and I could justify the separations was knowing that souls would be saved.

So often, even today, an excruciating schedule lies before me. Sometimes I'm still gone from home for weeks at a time. Thankfully, Pat is with me a good part of the time. But physically, so much travel is taxing. Emotionally, it is exhausting. Sometimes acquaintances suggest globe-trotting must be rather glamorous. Glamorous it is not!

Pat and I especially agonized before I left late in 1970 for Peru. The nation was standing at the brink of a leftist takeover. Even though guerilla warfare and bloodshed were the order of the day, our team had been invited to hold a large evangelistic crusade in the capital city. Preparations were in full swing. The local committee had invited me to come and preach at some pre-crusade rallies. I felt compelled to make a move before the situation got any worse. The trip proved to be an appointment with destiny, even though I wouldn't personally meet Rosario Rivera until years later.

Rosario's story

Rosario was born out of wedlock in the slums outside Lima, Peru. She grew up filled with anger at the lack of food and water and the destitution all around her.

Although she never finished her formal education, Rosario became an avid reader. By age thirteen she was reading Marx and Lenin. By eighteen she had become a militant communist.

While training in Cuba, Rosario met famed revolutionary Che Guevara and became his assistant. He filled her with a passion for her country and humanity.

Before Che Guevara went on a mission to Bolivia, he asked Rosario to survey the situation for him. But when she warned him not to go to Bolivia, he ignored her advice and met a violent death.

But death was nothing new to Rosario. She hated the upper

classes and whomever else stood in her way, and she spilled their blood without remorse during her missions.

Rosario returned to Lima on one particular mission in December 1970. She had become a bitter, angry, calloused woman who hated anything to do with God or Christianity.

When Rosario heard one of my daily Spanish radio programs and found out I would be speaking live at a theater that evening, she became enraged. Even though she didn't know me from Adam, she hated my guts.

During my message I spoke about the "Five Hells of Human Existence"—murder, robbery, deceit, hypocritical homes, and hatred. Each sin I mentioned pricked Rosario's conscience. When I gave the invitation, Rosario came forward with scores of other people. She wasn't thinking of conversion; murder was on her mind.

A little old lady, a Peruvian sister, saw Rosario standing there. So she went up and said, "Madam, can I help you receive Christ?" Rosario smacked the poor counselor, then panicked at the commotion she caused and ran from the theater.

21

As Rosario Rivera tossed and turned that night, God impressed two verses from my message on her mind. Jeremiah 17, verse five, reads, "Cursed is the one who trusts in man, who depends on flesh for his strength and whose heart turns away from the LORD." In contrast, verse seven says, "Blessed is the man who trusts in the LORD, whose confidence is in him."

Very early that morning, Rosario fell on her knees a hardened criminal, and stood back up a child of God. The Lord absolutely revolutionized this Marxist guerrilla, and today she is an amazing testimony of the transforming power of the Word of God.

Her communist comrades came looking for her. "I machine-gun them with Scriptures," she said. "Then when they leave, I thank God that His Spirit will work in them. The day they know our Lord, they will be the most valiant Christians in Latin America."

Twenty-five years later, Rosario is still a revolutionary, but now by the power of the Spirit of God. "If my heart burned for the revolution in the past, then it burns even more now, and if I did a lot for the poor before, then I do more now." The poor neighborhood where she came from, for instance, now has running water and electric lights, thanks to her efforts.

Rosario addresses high school classes and debates political matters, showing that only Christ can meet man's deepest needs. Scores of young people have received Christ as a result of her ministry. She also meets with factory bosses and tells them to treat their employees fairly. "I warn them that Christ is over them" (Colossians 4:1). Her social concern and Christian love have challenged churches throughout Peru to move authoritatively into society with God's Word.

You can imagine my surprise when I read about Rosario's conversion in a German news service dispatch ten years after our crusade in Lima, and my delight to finally meet her during another crusade in Lima a few years later. It's been our team's privilege to help support her work among the poorest of the poor this past decade.

Marxist revolutions in Latin America and elsewhere have never transformed lives for the better. As Rosario's story illustrates, the only revolution that works occurs every time someone becomes a new creation in Christ. He alone changes lives for good here and now— and for all eternity.

Harnessing the media

I returned to Lima, Peru, a few months into 1971, not quite sure what to expect. The city's large bullring accommodated more than 103,000 people during our two-week crusade. Nearly 5,000 people made public commitments to Jesus Christ. A press conference—unheard of for anything evangelistic—drew forty-two newsmen to a city center hotel.

Previously Christians were either ridiculed by the media or— worse—ignored. Suddenly we were receiving nationwide news coverage, and excerpts from my messages were broadcast on fifty-five radio stations. What Billy Graham had been able to do in the United States, we finally had done overseas—harnessing the secular media to spread the Good News of salvation in Jesus Christ.

With such an avalanche of media coverage, we found we could reach even the highest levels of society. In Guatemala that same year, President Col. Carlos Arana Osorio asked for a personal interview. The result was a twenty-five-minute meeting to talk about how Christianity builds a nation. How? Primarily through changed individuals who in turn, in their own place and according to their social and educational positions, live a just, hard-working, and "love-your-neighbor" life.

We also met with the mayor of Guatemala City, with the U.S. ambassador to Guatemala, and with top military officers. In twenty-two days, I preached to nearly 130,000 people, with more than 3,100 trusting Christ as Savior!

News media throughout Guatemala clamored for interviews. The nation's leading newspaper provided exceptional coverage almost every day, even quoting Scripture. The manager openly wept when I talked about Christ during one interview. Some journalists wrote better sermons than I could have written in that kind of space. One radio interview I did was broadcast more than sixty times on eight separate national stations in a single day.

An English-speaking church in the city became so excited about the national impact of the crusade that they raised enough money to pay for ten weekly programs to be broadcast on secular television immediately following the crusade.

"This is God's hour of visitation, and we dare not let the new opportunities pass us by," I wrote to prayer partners and supporters back home.

"We are expecting great things from God. Let's praise Him together for what He will surely do. These are great days to be alive. Dangerous, but exciting. Fruitful, in spite of the confusion and problems. Days of harvest. A fleeting hour of opportunity for us to 'buy up' and to redeem. Praise God for what He is doing and is yet about to do!"

I added, "We are facing the whitest harvest field we have ever known. We must put in the sickle now. But you and I cannot do it alone."

By now, we were dreaming of creating a God-consciousness in every city, every nation where we ministered. We couldn't do it alone, that was for sure. But by harnessing the power of the media, we found virtually *everyone* could hear the Gospel. We had just proved that in both Lima and Guatemala City.

Frankly, it grieves me that so many Christians characterize the media as "the enemy." Yes, journalists on the whole admit they're rather liberal. Most don't see eye to eye with us on many issues. Many haven't darkened the door of a church since their wedding. But, if we'll give them half a chance, they'll do more good for the cause of Christ in one day than we could do in half a year.

In *The New York Times* recently, Russell Baker wrote about returning after a three-week vacation. Even though he's a syndicated columnist and professional news junkie, Russell went cold turkey during his vacation. He didn't touch a newspaper for three weeks. His first morning back at the office, Russell spent two hours buried in all the newspapers he hadn't had an opportunity to read yet. His conclusion? "Little of consequence really happens in three weeks."

When thousands of people start packing a bullring, arena, or stadium night after night to hear someone *talk*, the media sit up and take notice! Believe me, I'm no singer or entertainer. Oh, I can tell a story and I do have a sense of humor. But it's not every day that tens of thousands of people pack out a venue to hear someone talk about God and the Bible. When it happens, it's news in every sense of the word.

I believe in making myself available to every media outlet in a city, cultivating relationships with journalists, and making myself available for interviews whenever asked, if possible. Almost always, I turn those meetings into an opportunity to ask reporters about their own city. After all, who better to ask about the pulse of a metropolis?

I also believe in being as transparent as possible with the media. I welcome their tough questions. After thousands of interviews, I've fielded a vast number of questions. And I honestly believe my team and I have nothing to hide. We're not afraid of being tripped up, embarrassed, or suddenly exposed as a phony or fraud. With the apostle Paul we can say:

> We do not peddle the word of God for profit. On the contrary, in Christ we speak before God with sincerity, like men sent from God (2 Corinthians 2:17).

Journalists often are surprised by the hundreds of local volunteers who work so hard for so many months to prepare for our crusades. We're anything but fly-by-night. We only come to a city at the invitation of the Christian congregations in that city. And we work side by side with them, every step of the way. We work *with* the Church, *through* the Church, *for* the Church.

Most reporters are surprised how much our team has to offer to a city. We sponsor pastor's conferences, radio and television outreaches, business and professional luncheons, women's events, youth rallies, children's programs, relief efforts to benefit the underprivileged, translation for those who speak other languages, signing for the deaf. We offer training seminars in friendship evangelism, counseling, and follow-up. We even help churches establish and lead six-week nurture groups to care for new believers after a crusade.

Reaching an entire continent

"This is the hour of God in Spanish America!" became our watchword. "The twenty-three Spanish-speaking countries of Latin America are our parish," we told people, echoing the words of John Wesley. We were even reaching "closed" Cuba via radio.

Publicly, we announced our God-given goal, namely: "to preach Jesus Christ fully to 250 million Spanish-speaking people in the world within the decade, utilizing all communications media, so millions will be transformed into victorious Christians."

I'd always believed in dreaming great dreams, but never before had

I been so public about my goals. The backlash our team got from certain quarters astounded us. Some said it was ridiculous to propose reaching a continent for Christ. Others publicly attacked our methodology, implying it would bear no lasting fruit. I was incredulous. Were they blind? Hadn't they read church history? And couldn't they see what God was doing in our day?

I talked the situation over with my team members. When all is said and done, we decided what really stands the test of time is converted, transformed people. Let the so-called "experts" say what they will and write what they wish. We would go on and win souls to Christ! We'd had it with wishy-washy "consultations," "study papers," and the ever present "new strategies." We would continue to preach Jesus Christ in the power of the Holy Spirit.

It wasn't until much later in the decade that we could finally prove what we had long suspected: unbiblical forces were infiltrating the Spanish Church, but bitterly opposing any who attempted to change the status quo. Looking back, I'm glad we didn't know what all we were going up against.

22

The next year, 1972, we had a glorious crusade in San Jose, the capital of Costa Rica, though it proved to be the greatest test of our entire ministry to that point. Crusade director Galo Vasquez, one of our team members from Ecuador, went home in tears many nights. His work of reviving and mobilizing Christians in preparation for evangelism was unbelievably hard. We faced opposition and indifference every step of the way. But God poured out His best recompense: tens of thousands filled the bullring and more than 3,200 boys and girls, youth and adults were converted to Jesus Christ!

One of those converts was Raul Vargas. Like many young people, his home life was miserable—there was fighting, jealousy, adultery. He cried himself to sleep at night, feeling a deep loneliness in his soul.

One day Raul met some Christians who gave him a Spanish New Testament. He started to read it, not knowing God could fill the deep emptiness he felt within.

After work one evening, Raul saw a poster: "Today, Luis Palau. Free admission." He had no money for the bus, so he walked a mile to the Plaza de Toros. God spoke to his heart that night, even though he didn't make a decision. The next night, he returned to the bullring. I preached from 2 Corinthians 5:17, which says, "If anyone is in Christ, he is a new creation; the old has gone, the new has come!" When I gave the invitation, Raul was ready to come forward to publicly commit his life to Christ.

Nineteen years later, back in San Jose for another crusade, I met Raul. He's no longer a young man on the outside, but what vibrancy he exudes! He pastors Oasis de Esperanza, the largest evangelical church in Costa Rica. He's led hundreds of people to Christ.

After giving me a big Latin hug, he told me, "Luis, there at the Plaza de Toros the worldly Raul died—not overcome by a bull, but by God's Word!"

A few months later, we were back in western Guatemala for four back-to-back crusades over twenty-two days. It was like performing major surgery without anesthetic. Galo Vasquez "operated" on two pastors whose fleshly battles with each other threatened to derail the crusades. After the surgery? The Presbyterian pastor's son was married—to everyone's obvious astonishment—at the Baptist church. The pastors performed the ceremony together, publicly clearing the air.

Equally as serious, the crusade committee in one city told us, "The mayor is an open atheist. He'll never turn out for the crusade meetings, and it's no use even attempting an interview. He wouldn't accept." Their grim faithlessness grieved me.

More than one-third of the city turned out for the opening night of our crusade in Coatepeque. Guess who was meekly peeking over people's heads in the back? The so-called atheist mayor. "Would you like to step up and sit on the platform with the evangelist?" one of my team members asked.

"Why, yes!" he said grinning. "I certainly would."

"You know," he leaned over and told me as we sat on the platform together, "in all this city's history, never has a crowd like this ever gathered—not even when our President came out west."

"Would you like to address the crowd tonight?" I asked. You should have heard the welcome that mayor gave us. Then he asked us to come to City Hall to visit him the next day. He was absolutely open, wanting to know more about the Bible, concerned about the future of his three children, and as friendly as can be. Would that more atheists were like him!

I've seen it again and again over the years: the very individuals everyone considers "least likely" to ever trust Jesus Christ as Savior are often the most responsive to the Gospel. I'd rather talk to an atheist any day of the week than someone who never even stops to think, "Do I believe there is a God? Why or why not?"

Further ministry expansion

Just as we'd dreamed, Latin Americans were coming alive to the Gospel in an unprecedented way. Before I'd languished, wondering when my opportunity to do crusade evangelism would come. Now I lamented my inability to accept all the crusade invitations coming my way. There was a continent to win. Even with a team, I could do only so much. Before God, I began to cultivate associate evangelists within our team, men like Galo Vazquez, Ed Silvoso (who married my sister Ruth), Carlos Quiroa, Marcelino Ortiz, and other choice, gifted servants of God, many of whom now have their own ministries and teams.

We also started producing evangelistic Gospel films, which could be used as part of the outreach of local churches or by missionaries starting a new work. Our philosophy was: we can't bring 250 million Spanish people to a bullring to hear the Gospel, but we can take the same transforming message from a bullring to millions of people all across the continent.

In addition, we began testing the concept of doing media campaigns in cities where later we would have live crusades. Large posters in subway stations and other well-trafficked locations would announce our evangelistic television specials. During the programs, we'd offer a free evangelistic booklet, a copy of the Gospel of John, and a Bible correspondence course. Everyone writing in would receive the free materials, plus a visit from a member of a nearby church. Later, they'd be invited by the church to attend our live crusade meetings and to bring family members and friends. The result? The spiritual soil of a city is extra prepared, the seed is well sown, and the crusade harvest is multiplied. It's a lot of work, it's costly, but we still like to use this strategy whenever possible, if the local crusade committee has a vision for it.

Early in 1973, our team broadcast our first live *English*-language television programs as part of a unique back-to-back crusade along the Texas/Mexican border. We reached many diverse people groups throughout the greater McAllen/Reynosa area. Some were rich, some dirt poor; some on the Texas side spoke only Spanish, some on the Mexican side, especially the young people, were fluent in both Spanish and English. It was a study in contrasts, but when all was said and done, more than 1,100 Mexicans and Americans had trusted Christ as Savior.

A few weeks later, only one and a half months before we were scheduled to have a crusade in the capital of the Dominican Republic, guerrillas attempted to overthrow the government. The future of the crusade was in question. But crusade director John McWilliam and the local crusade committee believed that God would see things through. Believe me, we asked for a lot of prayer for wisdom and safety and protection.

The twelve-day crusade in Santo Domingo went forward as planned, and I'm so glad it did. Political figures—including a presidential representative—international banking leaders, and people of the arts, culture, and letters attended a special evangelistic breakfast at the main ballroom in the Hilton Embajador Hotel. Some 70,000 people attended the evening crusade meetings. And nearly 2,400 people publicly committed their lives to Christ.

We also had a smaller crusade in the Mexican town of Obregon. Rarely have my team members and I seen a place so hungry for the Word of God. Everywhere we moved about the city— in shops, stores, restaurants, even on the street—we were leading needy people to Christ right and left.

One bookshop owner sensed the God-consciousness sweeping the area and offered to place evangelistic books in his 102 bookshops all over the three northwestern Mexican states, opening up yet another avenue of sharing the Gospel with the masses.

In anticipation of upcoming crusades the next year, I also spoke at pastors' conferences and evangelistic rallies in Bolivia and Ecuador. The last leg of the first trip was made in a very old one-engine Cessna airplane. Never again! The missionary pilot and I prayed that floating piece of cardboard and single propeller up and over a massive range of rugged Andes mountains.

If you've flown in a single engine airplane, you know they get tossed up and down and side to side by every bit of turbulence. At times, I found myself sucking my breath to help us skim just over the top of massive, razor-sharp mountain ridges. To top it all off, the weathered Australian pilot into whose hands I'd committed my life muttered: "Do you think *I* like flying such a dangerous route in such a small plane? If my boss hadn't sent me, I never would have attempted it." Such reassuring words! I could have choked the missionary who had shoved me into that dilapidated plane.

Was it worth those ninety minutes of terror? Definitely! "I arrived at this conference flat on my face," one Bolivian pastor told me as we walked toward the dining room. "Two weeks ago, brother Luis, I was ready to quit the pastorate. I'd had it. Too much criticism, too many discouragements, too much sin in my life. . . ."

"And now, Don Carlos?" I probed. "Are you quitting, then?"

"Not on your life! Now I know what victory is all about. Now I see what I can do to equip the people in my church for ministry. Now I have the vision of a crusade to prepare for!"

Before the conference ended, another pastor publicly stated: "At last we've had a retreat where they actually thought of us—as pastors." That was precisely our objective.

Another spoke up: "Yes, and it wasn't an imported philosophy they gave us. They speak our language! They understand us! They're Bolivians!" That last comment said a lot, considering the four conference speakers represented four countries other than Bolivia. But everything we talked about, everything we said was fitted to their situation.

It was wonderful to take a jumbo jet as we flew on to Ecuador, 1,600 miles away, for yet another pastors' conference, and then back to Mexico City to celebrate Christmas with Pat and the boys. I couldn't help looking out the window during each flight and thinking, *I love those big wings!*

As 1973 drew to a close, Pat and I reminisced about our first ten years on the mission field. How much had happened since the end of our first term in Colombia, let alone since our first rather difficult Christmas in Costa Rica back in 1963.

The most exciting days, however, were still ahead.

I n my Christmas letter of 1973, I wrote to our prayer partners and supporters: "We want to have bigger and better crusades. When it comes to conversion, our team philosophy is: 'The more the better.' There never can be too many people saved!"

With that in mind, we pursued an aggressive evangelistic television campaign after the first of the year. During Easter 1974, we reached millions of viewers in fifteen Latin American countries, plus Spain. Each of the eight nights of broadcasts coincided with the Holy Week observance of that day.

Unlike the commercialization we see here in the United States, holidays are a deeply religious time for many throughout Spain and Spanish America. Catholicism is an integral part of the cultural heritage for many. Granted, many are "Christian" in name only and rarely attend church. But when Easter and Christmas roll around, it's as if someone throws a switch. Otherwise secular people suddenly start thinking about God and the church, about sin and their need for God's forgiveness. What a prime time to give them the Gospel!

Presidential prayer breakfast

Actually, during 1974, it almost didn't matter how or when or where we proclaimed the Gospel. It's always relevant. Our first stop that spring was Bolivia, hit by 100 percent food price increases, riots, a presidential cabinet crisis with three ministers resigning, a massive rainstorm and flooding, and a "disaster area" proclamation—all the week we were supposed to have that nation's first Presidential Prayer Breakfast in La Paz, the capital.

Speaking to 125 dignitaries, including Bolivian President General Hugo Banzer, the Bolivian Secretary of State, the Chief Justice of the Supreme Court, the Air Force Chief of Staff, and the mayor of La Paz, I took up the theme of crisis and challenged the president and his guests to "Never give up the battle for righteous government."

From Scripture, I showed that it's impossible to govern a nation without God (2 Chronicles 7:14), that prayer is talking to God (John 16:24), and that to be heard by God, "we must be on God's side" (to quote Abraham Lincoln), meaning we must be born again (John 3:3-5).

Then I prayed for Bolivia. President Banzer was evidently touched by the Lord through it all. Afterward, he asked what he could do to help us reach his nation with the Gospel. I told him about our plans to return to his country that fall for three back-to-back evangelistic crusades (during which a phenomenal, record-breaking 9,210 people trusted Christ!). I then asked for—and the president authorized—ten nights of free air time on national television, starting that very evening.

On the way over to the television studios, I chatted with the Rev. Chester Schemper, South American director of The Bible League. As the well-preserved taxi lurched forward, I told Chester, "What we really need is 3,000 of your New Testaments to give away to the TV viewers."

"And who's going to pay for them?"

"All your rich American supporters!" I joked.

The program that night was our normal live call-in counseling format. The first caller, a thirty-year-old father of three whose wife had walked out, was desperate for answers. Right there on the air, I led him to Christ and offered him—and anyone else who phoned in—a free copy of the New Testament.

The following morning, President Banzer called with a rather stunning request. "I was watching Palau last night," he told a missionary friend of mine, David Farah, who served in Bolivia. "If you can get me one million copies of the New Testament, I will pass them on to the Ministry of Education. Instead of having catechism classes, we will have everyone studying the New Testament." David told me what the president had said. We both talked to Chester. It was a huge step of faith, but The Bible League accepted the challenge. As a result, since 1975 every primary and secondary school child in Bolivia has studied the New Testament twice a week!

Then it was on to Netzahualcoyotl, a brand-new metropolis outside Mexico City that, in less than a decade, had become the fourth largest city in the country. A huge "canvas cathedral" was filled to capacity all week, with more than 1,400 committing their lives to Christ. To our utter amazement, two-thirds of the converts were teenage boys and men.

During that crusade, Dr. Oscar Loya, the municipal president of Netzahualcoyotl, a special appointee of Governor Hank Gonzalez, became the first high-ranking Mexican government official to publicly sit on an evangelistic crusade platform. His presence exemplified the tremendous strides Christianity had achieved in a few short years, from a despised and persecuted little band of born-again believers to a minority officially recognized and respected by the government.

The chairman of the publicity committee for the crusade had become a Christian only four years earlier, during our historic 1970 Mexico City crusade. He was now pastoring a thriving 100-member church he had started himself.

From Netzahualcoyotl, it was back to Ecuador for a three-week crusade in the capital, Quito. The "Quito for Christ '74" crusade started so slowly that after the first five days, I called an executive crusade committee meeting to announce we were canceling the third week. The local committee clobbered me, exhorting and forcing me to consent to go the whole way.

As a team we shook our heads afterward for giving in to their pressure to go on. But by the end of the crusade we were glad we had stuck it out! The Bible Society sold out its entire inventory of 10,000 Spanish Bibles and 7,000 New Testaments a week before the crusade ended. Attendance climbed to 10,000 some nights, and 3,120 registered their decision to follow the Lord. Nine out of ten decision-makers had not heard the Gospel previously.

In addition, it was gratifying to work side by side with HCJB once more, broadcasting all three weeks of the crusade meetings "live" on radio to the rest of the continent. At the instructions of her psychiatrist, one woman took a jet flight from the coastal city of Guayaquil specifically to receive Christ. Team member Jim Williams counseled her that afternoon, she responded to the Gospel invitation at the crusade meeting that evening, and flew home the next day a "new creation" in Christ.

While in Quito, I also had an opportunity to meet with Ecuador's president, General Guillermo Rodriguez Lava, who warmly received us. I gave him a Spanish *Living New Testament*, Billy Graham's *World Aflame*, and a Bible commentary handbook.

During the crusade, it was exciting to see my little revolutionary friend, Maria, again and hear how she was still living for the Lord, as bold as ever.

As it turned out, another revolutionary came to Christ while we were there in Quito. He had heard me at the university, where I had a debate before eight hundred students. This communist leader was impressed by my "guts" to do such a thing and intrigued enough to come to the coliseum that evening, where he heard God's Word, received the Lord on the spot, and was saved.

"He is having grave persecution problems, as you can imagine," an HCJB missionary wrote to Pat and me later that year, "but he is going on with God."

A few weeks later I gave my testimony at Billy Graham's Phoenix, Arizona, crusade, the first of many such appearances I've been asked to make at his English-language crusades. About this time I also had my first two books published in English and Spanish.

First European crusade

Then it was on to Spain, birthplace of my father, for our team's first European crusade. We came at the invitation of the city of Sevilla's six evangelical churches for the first public evangelistic crusade in the city's more than 2,000-year history. The Inquisition had started there five centuries earlier; religious freedom had been the law of the land for less than eight short years, mainly as a stepping stone for Spain's entry into the European Common Market. Missionaries had sown the Word for decades, mostly on rocky soil. In a city of 750,000, less than 500 claimed to be born-again.

We knew the going would still be tough in Sevilla, but praised God when more people came to Christ each night of the crusade than had received Christ in many years.

I even had an opportunity, partway through the crusade, to meet with the mayor of Sevilla. Wanting to take full advantage of the opportunity, I presented him with a replica copy of the first Spanish translation of the Bible by Casiodora de Reina during the Reformation at the nearby San Isidro Convent. (This translation, since revised, is still popular in Spain and many other countries.) I even went so far as to propose that a statue of Casiodora de Reina should be erected in Sevilla in honor of his part in Spain's religious history. Amazingly, the mayor seemed to support the idea.

That evangelicals would be received openly by Sevilla's mayor was an historic breakthrough. So religious freedom had come to Spain, after all!

Two social police insisted on seeing me privately, however, after the closing night of our five-day crusade. The larger of the two was as big as an All-Pro defensive lineman. *What now?* I thought.

"Look," the bigger guy told me, "the city of Sevilla needs this message very, very much. But the next time you come, we'll get you the bullring. The whole city must hear it. We'll get you the people!" Quite a different response than I'd expected, I must confess.

Afterward, our team flew to the capital, Madrid, for the First Iberian Congress on Evangelization. We were heavily involved in the congress, afterward called the most strategic event in the history of the Iberian Church to that point.

That fall I flew to San Juan, Puerto Rico, at the request of HCJB to tape twenty-one five-minute television specials entitled *Luis Palau with Christmas News*. After covering part of the Christmas story as if it were breaking news, I then presented the Gospel message and offered a free evangelistic booklet. The programs aired in nearly a dozen countries that December, generating much positive response and many decisions for Christ. The programs were so successful that they were rebroadcast in subsequent years all across Latin America.

Plans for an even more aggressive broadcast strategy, *Continente '75*, were just around the corner. But first I had to answer the call to return to Europe.

I have been honored to speak at various national Christian conferences throughout the years, including the first major Promise Keepers conference held in Boulder, Colorado. [1992]

Since 1966, our evangelistic team has shared the Gospel of Jesus Christ via radio and television with hundreds of millions of people in ninety-five nations, as well as face-to-face with more than 11 million people on six continents.

Our crusade ministry is officially launched! [Bogotá, Colombia, December 1966]

During youth night in Fort Worth, a young gang member (left) turns his life over to Jesus

Food for the Hungry presented its 1992 Two Hungers award to Luis Palau for having "influenced the physical well-being of millions of people through his work in the spiritual realm." [Phoenix]

A radio interview with Dr. James Dobson (right front) ten years ago prompted Congressman Jim Talent of Missouri to commit his life to Jesus Christ.

People all over the world are searching for hope, for joy, for meaning. We long to introduce them to Jesus Christ!

Hundreds of thousands participated in a parade and rally in Mexico City on the final day of our 1992 Festival of the Family.

More than 340,000 attended our 1990-91 crusade meetings in Romania and 85,600 made public commitments to Jesus Christ.

Many people trust Jesus Christ during our live, call-in television counseling program, *Night Talk with Luis Palau*.

Over the course of fourteen weeks in 1983-84, we reached 528,000 in London, England. One week of crusade meetings was aired via satellite to fifty English-speaking countries.

Rev. Billy Graham has been a good friend and mentor over the years. In 1989, he encouraged me to "get going" and help re-evangelize America in our generation.

We reach tens of millions of people every day through our radio programs in both English and Spanish.

Nothing helps people, young and old, more than introducing them to Jesus Christ. [Jamaica, 1993]

Our family at Andrew and Wendy's wedding (from left)—Steve, me, Patricia, Andrew, Wendy, Gloria, Keith, Michelle, Kevin. [1994]

Early the next year, 1975, I had the privilege of spending several more days with Billy Graham, interpreting for him in Mexico City, answering his questions about our team's ministry, praying together, and talking about the re-evangelization of Europe. In particular, we talked about the strategic importance of the upcoming Eurofest '75 youth congress. Our desire was to see that congress re-ignite the spark of out-and-out evangelism in a weary land.

Even though I had grown up in Argentina, my family's roots went back to England, France, Germany, Scotland, and Spain. I looked forward to working side-by-side with Billy Graham and Bishop Festo Kivengere of Uganda, challenging 8,000 young people from more than thirty nations to reclaim Europe in Jesus' name.

That spring Pat joined me for an extended nine-nation European tour to speak at "mini-fests" and build momentum for Eurofest '75. Then, three weeks before we were to leave for the congress in Brussels, Belgium, Pat suddenly had to have emergency surgery to remove her gall bladder and appendix. Her surgery was successful and her recovery fairly rapid, thank the Lord.

The biggest highlight that summer for our sons Kevin and Keith was personally meeting and talking with Billy Graham at Eurofest. During the congress, Bishop Kivengere and I gave the morning Bible exposition on alternate days. Each message was simultaneously translated into thirteen languages. In my messages, I emphasized the importance of personal holiness and national vision as prerequisites to a European revival that would turn the church and continent upside down, as in the days of John Wesley and George Whitefield.

Partway through the congress, Harvey Thomas, a member of the Graham team who was serving as general secretary for Eurofest, came to me. "Luis, we have a problem," he explained. He had originally planned on encouraging all 8,000 youth delegates to attend Sunday morning services at various local churches there in Brussels. While preparing a list of all the area churches, however, Harvey realized it would be impossible for the small number of churches to accommodate such a huge number of visitors. At the last minute, he decided to add a huge Sunday morning worship service to the congress schedule and asked me to give the message. I was glad to help.

Harvey more than repaid me for that small favor. Not only had he given me a platform into Western Europe by inviting me to speak at Eurofest '75, but he also arranged for me to return the next year for a "Ministry of Thanks" tour of Britain. His practical support and the encouragement of the rest of the Graham team were invaluable as we broke new ground.

I felt like our evangelistic team had received a clear-cut Macedonian call to minister in Europe, just as the apostle Paul and his team had nineteen centuries earlier (Acts 16:9-10). But at the same time there was still a continent to finish reaching back in South America.

Continente '75

That fall we pursued the most ambitious Christian communications network in history, pioneering the use of a COMSAT satellite and other technology to blanket the Americas with the claims of Christ. In a strategy called *Continente '75*, we broadcast the Good News on fifty-six radio stations (live) and more than 100 television stations (taped) from New York to Punta Arenas, Chile, the southern-most city in the world. In one fell swoop, we reached an estimated 80 million people in twenty-three countries with the Gospel, eclipsing everything we'd done the previous decade.

The setting for this massive broadcast outreach was a volatile twenty-two-day crusade in Managua, Nicaragua (before the Sandinistas toppled the government and took over the country after a bitter civil war). *La Prensa*, one of the capital city's two major daily newspapers, vigorously attacked our crusade, calling it a "campaign of conformity," challenging me to an open debate, and accusing me of being a CIA operative. The charges couldn't have been more politically explosive. Thankfully, the equally secular *Novedades* newspaper defended our character and gave mostly positive front page coverage to crusade news.

Near the end of the three-week crusade, a woman met me on my way into Managua's brightly lit 20,000-seat National Baseball Stadium. With tears in her eyes, she gave me a big Latin hug and thanked me for presenting the Gospel so clearly because her grandson, Danilo, had received the Lord several nights earlier. "The next morning he was so happy. He told me, 'Granny, I've got eternal life,'" she said. The next day, tragedy struck.

I had been preaching through the book of Romans those three weeks, but I changed the title of my message to "I'll See You in Heaven, Danilo," and told his story just the way his grandmother had told me. When I told how Danilo had been out delivering newspapers, they thought I was going to say he invited his neighbors to the crusade that night.

But I said, "Then a truck came along, and *pow!*"

Some 30,000 people gasped, "Ohhh. . . ." They were as shaken by Danilo's death as I had been. Then I moved right into John 14. It was a fantastic night, with many receiving Jesus Christ as Savior at the end of the service. In addition, millions heard that night's message via satellite and shortwave radio. We also released a Spanish film of that message, winning other thousands to Christ.

Years later, people told me they still remembered that night, whether they were at the National Stadium, heard it on the continent-wide radio broadcast, or saw the message on film.

From death came life. That's what the Bible is all about. Little Danilo did not die in vain. All told, more than 5,700 people went forward during the National Stadium meetings, making it the second most fruitful crusade in any one city up to that time. The first, of course, was our equally historic 1970 Mexico City campaign.

While we were in Managua, the city was still reeling from a devastating earthquake that had claimed more than 10,000 lives three years earlier. In fact, we almost didn't get permission to use the National Stadium because of the structural damage it had sustained during the quake.

In February 1976, another violent earthquake hit Central America. Guatemala's President Laugerud Garcia asked Billy Graham and me to fly by helicopter over the twenty towns and villages worst hit by the quake. He then temporarily lifted a ban against all non-emergency broadcasting and asked us to present a ten-minute message to the nation. "Right now, our people need words of hope, something to give them courage to face these next few days and months," he told us. Our two evangelistic associations immediately pledged to funnel financial aid, food supplies, and other relief to the nation.

The most remarkable part of the trip was the almost immediate action taken by Guatemala's Christians to help their neighbors before outside assistance arrived. Of the approximately fifty government-authorized local relief agencies operating in the disaster zones, forty-eight of them were church committees. Who would have heard of such a thing only five years earlier? That practical outpouring of Christian charity and love proved to be a powerful witness, helping further accelerate Guatemala's explosive church growth over the next few years.

Even in the face of natural disasters, political upheavals, economic crises, and opposition on many sides, it was clear that Latin America was turning to Christ. As we began the second half of our decade-long thrust to evangelize the continent, we found ourselves simultaneously preparing for crusades in seven Spanish-speaking nations.

During our eight back-to-back crusades in Yucatan Peninsula, Mexico, during the spring of 1976, the mayor of one city told me, flat out, "You'll never fill that bullring."

"Mr. Mayor," I replied, "we'll fill one-half, and God will fill the other half." Some 12,000 people crowded in the last night, packing the stands and three-quarters of the Merida bullring grounds—everything except the area reserved for inquirers. More than 430 people committed their lives to Jesus Christ that night!

As in other regions, our ongoing daily radio ministry prepared the way for a tremendous harvest of souls. Meeting with the assistant to the governor of Yucatan, I learned he happened to tune in our program on his car radio on the way to the airport several months earlier. Since then, he had been an avid listener.

Despite the strict Mexican law of separation of church and state, in six of the eight cities the mayors received us as official visitors. In three of those cities, the mayor actually sat on the crusade platform with me at least one of the nights. In Ticul, the local priest who had been against the crusade changed his mind and, at the last minute, posted a sign on his church door: "No mass tonight—go hear Palau."

Festival of the Family

In Chiclayo, Peru, a new church that already had one hundred fifty members grew seven hundred percent in less than a week through a carefully planned church growth effort. Working with Christian Brethren missionary Bill Conard, who later joined our team, we held a five-day crusade.

Instead of calling it a "United Christian Campaign" or "Crusade with Luis Palau," we experimented with the name "Festival of the Family." During the day, we conducted seminars and workshops on family issues. For four nights we also broadcast our live television counseling program on Channel 4, answering a host of questions on family and spiritual issues. And then for three nights we held meetings in the city's Plaza de Armas. All told, just over 800 people received Jesus Christ by Saturday, and 1,000 showed up for church Sunday morning!

That same weekend I flew to Bogotá, Colombia, where we saw 1,150 of 24,000 people in attendance Saturday and Sunday evening trust Christ. Never before had I seen so many respond to the Gospel outside the context of a full-scale crusade since our first such crusade ten years earlier in this same city.

Ten years! Was it only such a short time ago that Dick Hillis and the OC board had given me the green light to pursue full-time crusade evangelism? As I walked the streets of downtown Bogotá, I reflected on all that had happened the previous decade and wondered, *What lay ahead?*

25

A few weeks later, I took a break from our all-out efforts in Latin America for my first full-fledged United Kingdom tour. I traveled to thirteen cities in four nations over a two-week period.

"You cannot imagine what a joy and a privilege it is for me to visit the United Kingdom, to minister from the Word of God, to tell of His work in Latin America, and to say 'thank you' to British Christians for their faithfulness in sending the missionaries who led my family and me to Jesus Christ," I told an overflow crowd at the Millmead Centre in Guildford, as I finished the tour.

After hearing me speak at St. Paul's Church in London a few days earlier, a retired missionary to Peru recalled a prophetic conversation in that country at the turn of the century: "The day will come when Third World missionaries will return to bring the Gospel to a post-Christian Britain."

The warm reception I received throughout the "Ministry of Thanks" tour and the invitations Christian leaders extended for me to return for major citywide crusades were gratifying. So Europe was opening up to me, a Third World evangelist, after all! In my heart, I was as committed as ever to evangelize Latin America. But I was convinced God was calling me to help re-evangelize the British Isles, as well. The two goals were complementary, not contradictory, to my way of thinking. After all, hadn't Keith Bentson taught me to pray for the world? And hadn't John Wesley once said, "The world is my parish"? Why shouldn't it be my parish, as well, if God so led?

Appointed OC's new president

As it turns out, my mission, OC International, had that in mind for me, too. That summer, on the twenty-fifth anniversary of the founding of the mission, Dick Hillis asked the OC board to appoint me to succeed him as president. Only sixty-three at the time, Dick wanted to continue working closely and actively with the mission for many more years. But it was time, he said, to hand over the reins. That he would turn it over to me was unprecedented.

It was the first time someone from the Third World had ever been named president of a U.S.-based missions agency. In some ways, Dick Hillis was making a point that missions expert Patrick Johnstone and others would later document: that the whole church (not just the Western church) was rising up to reach the whole world with the whole Gospel in our generation.

After receiving assurances from Dick and the other OC board members that my new responsibilities would in no way hinder my evangelistic ministry, I accepted the challenge. I was forty-one at the time and anxious not to lose any momentum.

Most evangelists burn out after five or ten years, for one reason or another. It's not always pride or sex or money that does them in; more often, they just get tired and give up. Oh, they may go on to head a worthy ministry or go into full-time Bible teaching, which I'd love to do. But whatever the reason, they stop doing crusade evangelism. Not that quitting was an option at the moment! God was opening fantastic doors of opportunity to reach the masses with the claims of Christ. I wanted to be faithful to my calling.

Revival in Paraguay

A few days after accepting the presidency of OC International, I was on my way to Asunción, Paraguay, for what proved to be one of the most exciting crusades in our team's history. Over the course of twelve days I spoke to more than 100,000 people, including a private meeting with President Alfredo Stroessner. More than 4,900 committed their lives to Christ as a result of our evening crusade meetings, affinity group meetings, and counseling ministries.

During the crusade up to seventy people at one time lined up outside our crusade Family Counseling Center waiting to talk to someone. I vividly remember one couple, both barely thirty. The husband was an attorney, the brother of a doctor who served on the crusade committee. As we sat together, their very appearance made me sad. Eyes downcast, neither would look at each other or directly at me. They were terribly embarrassed, yet something had driven them to come for help.

His attitude was typically Latin. He had been unfaithful, committing immorality since his university days. He never thought of the hurt he caused his wife.

Then, his wife began taking classes at the university. A friend of her husband's became coyly friendly—sympathizing with her, "You poor thing, so beautiful, so young, and your husband is fooling around behind your back" (you can guess the old line).

The outcome was predictable. Soon the wife, too, fell into adultery. Now, here they sat before me, both ashamed, miserable, looking for a solution to their dilemma. What suffering I saw in their faces!

We talked together and read God's Word. Then I made them confess everything to each other—every single thing. Tears began to flow as the three of us knelt together. Impulsively they embraced as they asked God to forgive them. They then turned to each other and asked for forgiveness. That broke me up right there!

Compassion for souls

To keep doing the work of an evangelist always demands that I keep alive and burning a compassion for souls—to be ready to weep and cry for the suffering through which others are going.

Why did the Lord have "compassion" on people? Because they "fainted," they were "harassed," they were "weak and pushed around." That same situation is so true in Latin America, and other parts of the Third World, and even in Europe and America today—in spite of all the facades of strength and sophistication.

When you begin talking directly to people about their problems, you realize how much they suffer without Jesus Christ in their lives. That's why I've always made myself available to do counseling personally and over the air with our live television call-in program.

One rather famous comedian in Paraguay watched me counsel people on television and decided to host a mock call-in show mimicking me on another station. As he repeatedly listened to tapes of our counseling programs, however, while strenuously trying to learn how to imitate my mannerisms, the message of the Gospel started sinking in. Instead of mocking Christianity, he ended up giving his life to Jesus Christ!

At the end of our crusade in Paraguay's capital, a representative of President Stroessner told us at the airport, "*Conquistaron!*" (You conquered!). Actually, the Lord conquered that city and nation for Christ. The evangelical population more than doubled in less than two weeks, we were told by church historian Rogelio Duarte.

Rosario plan

From Asunción, Paraguay, it was on to Rosario, Argentina—about the last place I ever wanted to have a crusade. At the time, Rosario was a volatile industrial city of more than 1 million people, boasting one of the world's first nuclear power generating reactors. It had a reputation for Roaring Twenties-style, gangster-like bombings, kidnappings, and murders in broad daylight. Worse, the city was spiritually weak and divided.

Done in the power of the Holy Spirit, mass evangelism unites Christians like nothing else can. But was it possible for Rosario's churches to come together? For months, it looked hopeless. The forty churches scattered throughout that huge city were ingrown, for the most part. Pastors struggled, congregations languished.

If it had been up to me, I would have turned down the invitation to go to Rosario in a minute. But team member Ed Silvoso was absolutely convinced that God was about to turn the city upside down spiritually.

Slowly and carefully, working with Dr. Donald McGavran, Peter Wagner, and Leighton Ford, Ed developed a comprehensive plan that united church growth principles with proved crusade evangelism strategies. As I reviewed the "Rosario Plan," as it came to be called, my own heart was stirred.

It had taken ninety years of missionary activity to plant forty churches, none of which had more than 200 members. The "Rosario Plan" envisioned the planting of fifty new churches in eighteen months, churches that would be ready to receive new members during and immediately after a two-week evangelistic crusade.

In the past, we'd seen scores of churches started after our crusades all across Latin America. Ed's point was, *Wouldn't we see even more people going on for the Lord a year later if we had new churches all ready for them to join the week they came to Christ, instead of making them wait a few weeks or months?*

And, *Wouldn't we see more churches planted if we developed a strategic plan for such growth?*

Church Growth seminars were held. Nearly seventy of the city's pastors and church leaders enthusiastically adopted the Rosario Plan. Two basic hurdles were identified.

First, the work of evangelism in Rosario, up to that time, had been left almost entirely to the pastors. One commented, "My congregation feels this is what they pay me for."

Second, the pastors admitted they had become almost completely preoccupied with the activities of their churches, leaving little or no time to even think about evangelism.

We challenged the pastors to begin training their people in personal evangelism and fulfilling their scriptural responsibility to "prepare God's people for works of service" (Ephesians 4:12).

The results were amazing. These same pastors soon were reporting a new vibrancy in their churches. One pastor had already written his letter of resignation after months of discouraging church decline. The next thing we knew, his congregation had won sixty-five people to Christ and was bursting at the seams.

Soon the vision of these pastors surpassed our own! Thirty-five home-based churches were planted. Then, during our November 1976 crusade, more than 4,500 people committed their lives to Christ, doubling the number of Christians in a fortnight. In addition, more than 110,000 homes throughout the city were visited, and other hundreds of thousands heard the Gospel via radio and television.

Did the Rosario Plan work? Perfectly, no. It was only a prototype of even more effective evangelism we'd do in the future, including an updated version of the plan we used a year and a half later in Uruguay. But extensive post-crusade research showed that fifty-four percent of the new converts were incorporated into local churches and were still going on for the Lord many months after the crusade ended.

Even more exciting, thirty of the thirty-five new churches were thriving three years later, nearly doubling what had previously taken almost a century to accomplish.

26

The week after Christmas, it was my privilege to join Elizabeth Elliot, Billy Graham, Helen Roseveare, and John Stott speaking to 17,000 university students at the Urbana '76 missions conference.

The twin themes of Urbana were suffering and "declaring God's glory among the nations." The latter theme was based on Psalm 96, one of my favorite Old Testament missionary Scriptures.

The other theme wasn't planned. But when Elizabeth Elliot quoted one of the letters her husband Jim wrote before his martyrdom ("if we are the sheep of His pasture, then we are headed for the altar")—and British missionary Helen Roseveare, M.D., told of going through weeks of absolutely unthinkable atrocities and personal humiliations beyond description at the hands of rebel soldiers in Zaire, Africa, 1964, for the sake of Christ—I was shaken and humbled. Once again I was forced to ask myself, *Am I willing to serve God no matter what?*

It was so good to see Billy Graham again and talk with him about the future of mass evangelism. And John Stott and I talked about our team's upcoming crusade in Wales that next summer.

As we crossed the threshold into a new year, Dick Hillis and I talked about my evangelistic team's plans for 1977. If Ray Stedman was my spiritual father when I came to America, Dick was my uncle. He worked hard to cultivate the leadership gift he saw in me, emphasizing the importance of multiplication (2 Timothy 2:2) and learning by example. He also stressed gaining a vision for something bigger than yourself.

Dick confirmed what I had observed: culturally, most Americans tend to be inward focused. We get so caught up in the present moment that we have no concept of the big picture, of what God is doing and wants to do here in this country and around the world.

Even though my growing burden and dreams for winning the world to Christ were stretching OC International further than it had even been stretched as a mission before, Dick kept encouraging me and building an even larger platform under me.

No dream was too big, in his thinking.

Pressures of ministry

At times, I had second thoughts. Even with someone like Dick cheering you on and a dedicated team working right there with you, trying to win cities and nations and continents to Christ is overwhelming.

Because our team has preparations for fifteen or twenty crusades under way at any given time, and because we've worked in so many different places over the years, just about any international news I hear or read has a direct bearing on our plans for world evangelism. An earthquake or political upheaval or economic tremor "somewhere" means something! Often, it's easy for me to get worked up about world events and neglect the next thing on the to-do list right in front of me. Correspondence and phone calls can wait. But how will this crisis or that natural disaster affect our upcoming crusade plans?

Not that my staff ever notice these tendencies, of course! One day one of the secretaries slipped into my office while I was at lunch. When I came back, there was a little sign on my desk. "For peace of mind, please resign as manager of the universe."

She was right. I can get too worked up sometimes. It's all too easy to take on burdens no one is asking us to take on, not even God. On the other hand, when I'm dead tired and my schedule's overloaded and I'm tempted to complain about doing one more television call-in program or one more radio interview or one more speaking event, it's almost as if the voice of the Lord starts saying, "Oh, you are tired, are you? Do you want Me to take away this opportunity and that opportunity and trim back your crusade schedule and let you start twiddling your thumbs waiting for something to do? Just give Me the word."

When that happens, I panic! I have almost an out-and-out dialogue with God, right on the spot. "No, Lord, forgive me for even thinking about complaining. I love to be Your ambassador, and I'm ready for my next assignment."

After all, God doesn't owe me anything. He's not obligated to keep using me. My ministry could be over in a minute if the Lord so chooses. Everything I do and everything I am is thanks to His mercy and grace. Like John Wesley, George Whitefield, Charles Finney, D. L. Moody, Billy Graham, and others before me, I want to be found faithful to Christ to the end.

During the spring of 1977, I had the privilege of ministering in Germany and then returning to Argentina for an explosive youth crusade in Buenos Aires, where we saw 3,000 come to Christ in less than a week. While there, I heard further reports about the ongoing impact of our "Rosario Plan" crusade to the north.

Back to childhood roots

I also made a pilgrimage back to Ingenero-Maschwitz, where my family had lived before my father's death and our subsequent bankruptcy thirty years earlier. I was asked to preach in the very chapel that my dad had built and that I had attended during most of my childhood.

I had a lump in my throat as I saw my little nephews—who looked so much like me when I was a boy—sitting on the pews. When we sang one of my father's favorite hymns, about the joy of bringing other sheep into Christ's fold despite manifold trials, I could hardly go on. So many memories and emotions flooded in, all at once. When my father died, I was still a lost sheep, wandering from God. He never had the joy of seeing me turn to Christ, let alone watching me follow in his footsteps, leading still other sheep into the family of God.

When I received an honorary doctorate of divinity degree from Talbot Theological Seminary, La Mirada, California, a few days later, I publicly thanked God for the men He had brought into my life, after my father's death, who spiritually nurtured, discipled, trained, and equipped me to serve the King of kings.

"If they had not come to Argentina," I said, "if they had not loved me, if they had not gotten close to me and prayed with me and encouraged me to get on with the Lord's work, I might still be in Argentina, still in that little chapel . . . doing nothing for the Lord."

While I might not have all the formal education some have, I thank God for men like George Mereshian, Keith Bentson, and others who came to Argentina and taught me so much, on our knees in the Word of God and on our feet praying for the nations.

"God has no grandchildren"

Not that I've ever stopped learning, by any means. While in

Cardiff, Wales, for a crusade that summer, retired Welsh missionary David Morris taught me another valuable lesson I'll never forget.

"God has no grandchildren," he told me. "Every generation must experience its own spiritual awakening. I left my land in a state of revival. I returned fifty years later, in my old age, to find it paganized, secularized, and desperately needy of another touch from God."

Paganized it was. I'd never seen anything like it anywhere else in the world. At every pub and sporting event, the Welsh—who love to sing—were packing down pints as if they were going out of style while singing Gospel hymns with all the gusto they could muster. They absolutely loved the old hymns of the faith. But they simply did not know Jesus Christ.

There in Wales, British pop star Cliff Richard and I first teamed up. Cliff made a deal with me: he wouldn't preach if I didn't sing. I kept my end of the bargain, and rejoiced to hear Cliff so clearly articulate the Christian faith he had made his own a few years earlier.

Cliff Richard's songs air all the time here in the U.S., but he's *the* biggest rock 'n roll superstar in British history and has been since his late teens. Others have come and gone. After more than twenty-five years at the top, Cliff is still number one.

Together, Cliff and I made an evangelistic film that was greatly used of the Lord on both sides of the Atlantic. We also talked of teaming up again, which we've since done many times. Cliff draws a crowd like few others can and puts out the Gospel better than most. His specialty is apologetics, articulating why Christianity is relevant and true.

Seventeen years later, we're still hearing testimonies of people converted during our Jubilee '77 crusade in Cardiff, Wales. Part of the reason is because the British are such good letter writers. It may take them years, but they'll always get around to writing you to thank you for leading them to Christ. Believe me, I save every letter!

One young woman admitted she came to hear Cliff Richard sing, stayed to hear my message, and was converted that night. Another young woman—a member of the Jehovah's Witnesses—came to Christ. Later, through her witness, most of the rest of her family received Christ, as well. One young man was in Cardiff visiting relatives. He heard we needed more ushers, volunteered to help, heard the Gospel, and was saved. Later, he went into television and helped us get the Word out when we returned to Wales for another crusade twelve years later.

All told, nearly 1,600 committed their lives to Christ. When local pastors asked me how the crusade compared to the harvest we'd seen in Latin America, I told them about the early days, when we first started out. There were small numbers of conversions. It was mostly a time of plowing hardened soil and planting the seed of the Gospel. Some harvesting, to be sure, but much, much more to come!

In Latin America, the harvest was indeed plentiful. When we returned for a crusade in the Dominican Republic that fall, *Time* magazine gave us unprecedented coverage. The journalist, a veteran with years of experience in Latin America, reported the facts: crowd size (105,000), number of decisions (nearly 4,000), my preaching style, that sort of thing. But he also saw beyond the crusade itself, something I wish more writers did! He concluded his report by observing:

Colombian Novelist Rómulo Gallegos once wrote of Latin America: "She loves, she suffers, she waits." Palau believes this well portrays a continent where people depend on luck and feel that "some day something is going to break." Also, in Palau's view Latin America, with its emphasis on the Cross, is "oriented to a dead Christ. Our emphasis is that he is alive. He can touch your life now, revolutionize your home, make you a different person."

27

About the same time *Time* magazine was reporting on Latin America turning to Christ, the Gallup Poll was reporting one exception to the rule: Uruguay. Once called the "Switzerland of South America," it had become a nation adrift, searching for its soul. Some Uruguayans even wondered out loud if they had a soul. Fully thirty percent claimed to be atheists, unheard of anywhere else outside the communist world.

Atheists may make a lot of noise in America, but they constitute less than one percent of the population. Most non-religious people are actually agnostics who claim we can't know if God exists. Few are true atheists, adamant that God doesn't exist.

But in Uruguay, nearly one-third of the nation claimed "there is no God." The pervasiveness of communism and other atheistic and materialistic philosophies came as no surprise when we arrived for crusades in the capital, Montevideo, and five other key cities strategically located along Uruguay's western, southern, eastern, and northern borders.

Flying from city to city was out of the question, so my team members and I traveled together in a fantastic assortment of older cars (some that required more oil than gas) through 1,600 miles of Uruguayan roads (often dusty and sometimes overrun by herds of cattle) to present the Gospel to more than 100,000 men, women, and atheistic youth.

Leading atheists to Christ

Although the six back-to-back crusades were exhausting, we were jubilant at the response to the Gospel. During one of our live counseling programs on TV Channel 12, a woman told me flat out, "I'm an atheist."

"So, why are you calling me, then?" I asked.

"I want you to convince me, Palau. Sell me on God, please!"

Another woman heard me talking about family problems during

another program and couldn't stop watching. Her marriage was ending in divorce. She and her husband, Bario, hadn't slept together in five years. They wouldn't even eat together. In her misery Nancy cried out, "Lord, if it's true that You exist, why are these things happening to me?"

That night Nancy told her husband she was going tomorrow to the Palacio Penarol Stadium in Montevideo to hear me speak, then shuddered, realizing she had actually *talked* to Bario. They hadn't spoken to each other in ages. They both ended up going to the crusade and committing their lives—and marriage—to Christ.

"From that moment our lives have changed completely," Nancy told me later. "Every day we are surprised at how much we learn. We pray together, we share things together. . . . People say we aren't the same." Not surprisingly, within five months Nancy and Bario had led thirty-five souls to the feet of Jesus!

All told, more than 8,100 Uruguayans came to faith in Christ during the crusade meetings themselves. While thirty percent of the decision-makers reported some kind of religious background, fully seventy percent previously were unchurched. I decided then and there, *I like preaching to atheists!*

In some ways, atheists are intellectually dishonest. All creation shouts, "There is a God!" On the other hand, they aren't playing any pseudo-religious games. Even if they haven't found the right answers, at least they're thinking about life's big questions. We certainly saw that when the Lord opened up the door for us to preach in Hungary, Poland, Russia, and other communist countries a few years later.

After Uruguay, I was scheduled to take a whirlwind tour through Scotland, Germany, France, Wales, and England to speak at evangelistic rallies and pastors' conferences. But first I flew to OC International headquarters in California to meet with the board of directors. When Dick Hillis and the board had offered me the presidency in 1976, it was with the understanding that the situation would be reviewed in two years.

Starting a new organization

I had prayerfully reviewed the situation myself and felt compelled to ask the OC board to be freed from my responsibilities. In many ways, it was becoming impossible to manage my own thirty-member evangelistic team and give OC the leadership it needed and deserved.

As much as I loved OC and owed such a great debt to Dick Hillis, we all agreed it would be best if the Luis Palau Evangelistic Association (LPEA) became a separate missions organization, effective the first of October. They gave me their full blessing and unanimously requested that I continue to serve on the OC board. Dick also agreed to serve on LPEA's new board.

In five months, LPEA was on its own, with new headquarters in Portland, Oregon. Original board members included Paul Garza (construction contractor and former missionary to Spain), Dr. Hillis, Milton Klausmann (chairman of the American Aluminum Company), Duane Logsdon (president of Specialty Products Company and former pastor), Don Ward (financial planner), and myself. A little later, two other outstanding men of God—Dr. Ted Engstrom (executive director of World Vision) and Dr. Walter Smyth (vice president of international ministries for the Billy Graham Evangelistic Association)—joined LPEA's board, as well.

Given the pressures associated with launching an independent ministry, I thank God for the wisdom and experience and passion for souls each member brought to our board meetings in the late 1970s and into the 1980s. I'm also glad I didn't have to shoulder all the ministry burdens myself. The thought of bearing full responsibility to make sure all thirty (now more than sixty) members of the evangelistic team just get paid every month would be enough to sober anyone.

During this time a gentleman named David Hall heard me preach at Winnetka Bible Church. A successful businessman in the Chicago area, David thought he was doing quite well without the Lord, thank you. But the seed of the Gospel was planted in his heart, and he gave his life to Christ when I returned to present a week-long Bible conference a year later. Soon David and his wife, Kathleen, discovered that what had happened in his life was happening to others all over the world, and wholeheartedly started supporting our ministry. That was fifteen years ago. David now serves as chairman of LPEA's board of directors. Would that all converts had such a burden to see others won to Christ!

Huge revival in Bolivia

If there were reasons for concern those first few days after LPEA officially launched out on its own, they were immediately eclipsed a couple of weeks later in Bolivia. What a revival! We'd already reaped a plentiful harvest there four years earlier and received President Hugo Banzer's incredible request for one million Spanish New Testaments so every student in the country could study God's Word.

But nothing could have prepared us for the national revival we saw in October 1978. In the capital, La Paz, police had to close the stadium gates each night, turning hundreds of people away from our public crusade meetings. On Saturday and Sunday we held two services each afternoon and evening. The lines of people waiting to enter the stadium stretched for blocks. In Santa Cruz and Cochabamba the response also was overwhelming. The three weeks of meetings broke almost every crusade record we'd ever set—for attendance (180,000), decisions for Christ (18,916), and ratio of decisions to attendance (10.5 percent).

Numbers don't tell the whole story, of course. They only suggest how many stories *could* be told. Throughout Bolivia, conversion stories abounded. I'll never forget two conversions that were probably never even recorded on the crusade statistic sheets.

Journalists' pens were scratching away in one of the rooms of a prestigious La Paz hotel during a mid-morning press conference. I was providing ready answers to sometimes barbed questions from some of Bolivia's leading writers and editors when a little girl slipped into the room. I recognized her as the daughter of the hotel elevator operator. *What could she possibly want?*

I reached for a copy of one of my books, autographed it, handed it to the girl, whispered, "The Lord bless you, sweetheart," and smiled. But the little girl tenaciously held her ground.

A book and smile were not her goal. "Mr. Palau, what I really wanted to ask you was how I could receive Jesus in my heart."

That changed the picture rather quickly!

The previous evening this girl, who looked younger than her eleven years, had watched me counsel people on national television. I'd spoken to a high school student, leading him to Christ. Now she wanted to receive Him, too.

Quickly, the newsmen were asked to leave. Publicity is necessary and fine, but the rest of their questions would have to wait until another time. "*Now* is the day of salvation" (2 Corinthians 6:2, emphasis added).

Leading a president to Christ

That same week we held another Presidential Prayer Breakfast with Bolivia's new president, General Juan Pereda Asbun, twenty-five high ranking military officers, eight cabinet members, and many other leaders. In my twenty-minute address, I read Deuteronomy 28:1-14 and outlined the positive national benefits that result when a country obeys the Lord. In response, President Pereda stood up and reaffirmed the importance of setting "personal and national spiritual priorities" and publicly endorsed our crusades. Afterward, in a private meeting, I asked him about his own soul and explained the Good News of forgiveness through the blood of Jesus Christ. There in his presidential office, Pereda bowed his head and gave his life to Christ.

When you think about it, there's no greater thrill than leading someone to Christ. People often ask what I think about when I stand before a crowd and give the invitation for people to commit their lives to the Lord and then come forward. More often than not, I'm praying for that distraught couple sitting off to my left, whose eyes are full of tears and whose hearts are full of grief. I'm praying for the group of young people sitting directly in front of me toward the back, that God will open their hearts and change their lives tonight. I'm praying for the governor or mayor standing behind me on the platform, who needs Christ just as much as anyone else this evening.

My team and I returned from Bolivia jubilant! Never before had we seen so many from every walk of life give their lives to the Lord. We saw thousands more trust Jesus Christ a few weeks later in Acapulco and Veracruz, Mexico. To have three such successful crusades in a row after launching out on our own was a God-send.

In my heart, I felt God was reaffirming His call on my life and His blessing on our team. Not that it would be easy street from here on out, to be sure.

28

Speaking to university students on their turf always is a bit unnerving, but when communist radicals try to shout you down, you quickly start thinking about canceling your upcoming lectures in other universities.

In conjunction with Billy Graham's three-week crusade in Sydney, our team was invited to hold a crusade in Newcastle, one of Australia's other leading cities, during the spring of 1979.

In addition to evening crusade meetings at the Newcastle Showgrounds, my itinerary included a full schedule of media interviews and five university lectures.

The crusade meetings went well. Media coverage was quite extensive. But the university lectures almost didn't happen.

At the University of Sydney, we had a free-for-all. I was speaking to about 800 students on the mall about what Christ can do for a nation when a group of Marxist-Leninists began shouting obscenities at me.

I kept going, mentioning former U.S. Secretary of State Henry Kissinger's observation that there were no more than twenty-four free nations left in the world. One striking characteristic of those twenty-four nations: All had been profoundly influenced by evangelistic awakenings within the past two or three centuries. I then reminded the students that they were reaping the benefits of living in a nation that had been blessed because of its Christian roots.

Even if a nation was now pagan and in need of massive change, "there is only one revolution that works," I told the students, "and that's the revolution in the heart through faith in Jesus Christ."

Those remarks prompted one Marxist agitator (who looked rather like Fidel Castro in his younger days) to point his finger at me and shout gross obscenities. I tried to intelligently debate him, but all he knew were swear words, readily admitting he had no basis for his doctrine.

Only a few days earlier, back in England, I had been the keynote speaker at Spring Harvest, a national Christian youth congress. Instead of debating communism versus Christianity, 3,600 young people spent several days in in-depth Bible study, practical discipleship, and evangelism training. They ate it up, so much so that I was invited back for a second Spring Harvest congress the next spring. Attendance nearly tripled, and has kept growing ever since. (About 75,000 now attend the annual congress!)

Another breakthrough that spring was the sudden openings to get on local and national BBC radio and television, in conjunction with a month-long crusade in northeast Scotland. Once a land of reformers and other theological giants, the question of the hour now was, *Can Scotland be revived?*

"Aren't you trying to flog a dead horse?" one BBC newsman asked me. Another journalist asked why I was wasting my time on a post-Christian society.

"I don't believe there is any such thing as a post-Christian society," I replied. "Either a person is or isn't a Christian. One generation may reject the Gospel for itself, but each new generation does have the opportunity to make its own choice. I cannot accept that a society can exist where the Gospel is no longer relevant."

Arnold Toynbee, the great historian, once noted that most people don't reject Christianity, they reject a caricature. That was certainly the case in Scotland. Everywhere I looked, Scots were rejecting empty ritual and dead religion. Empty churches were boarded up. Only a small minority had experienced the reality of the resurrected, living Lord Jesus Christ. Few longed to see Scotland blessed by God once again.

As our team drove through the marvelously lush valleys of Scotland, my heart cried out for a fresh outpouring of the Holy Spirit upon the land where men of God such as John Knox, Robert Murray M'Cheyne, and Andrew Bonar once saw revival and the salvation of thousands of souls.

My crusade messages in Aberdeen were broadcast nightly throughout Europe and the British Isles on Trans World Radio's million-watt transmitter in Monte Carlo. But they made their biggest impact locally, as Scottish ministers started re-examining their own styles of preaching after seeing hundreds of people coming to

Christ, including nearly 1,000 teenagers. Afterward, we accepted an invitation from churches in half a dozen other parts of Scotland to return the next year for more evangelistic rallies and crusades, confident the winds of change had indeed begun to blow.

Back home, I had two teenagers of my own to counsel after a sixteen-year-old friend of theirs committed suicide. Together we went to see a film on death and dying at their local high school, then had a good talk afterward. No, the deceased don't just become a "memory," as the movie suggested. That's a romantic idea without any basis in reality. Scripture teaches that "man is destined to die once, and after that to face judgment" (Hebrews 9:27). By trusting in Jesus Christ, we can have our sins forgiven and know we're going to heaven.

I was glad both Kevin and Keith knew the Lord, though Pat and I longed to see them become more earnest for the things of God. Privately, we wondered whether they were becoming overly attracted by what the world has to offer.

The attraction of the world doesn't tug at only the young, however. That fall, three of my key team members and I traveled to Lima, Peru, for the second Latin American Conference on Evangelism (CLADE II), sponsored by the Evangelical Theological Fraternity of Latin America, which was born at CLADE I ten years earlier. Some 300 Christian leaders from twenty nations gathered for nine days to talk about evangelism. Incredibly, biblical evangelism was about the last thing anyone talked about during the conference. Much of the program stressed the temporal, rather than the spiritual. Many delegates complained about what they called the "socio-political content" of the majority of messages.

I had been invited to give a keynote address toward the end of the conference on "Evangelism in the Eighties: What Lies Ahead." Clearly, what I had planned to talk about countered the not-so-hidden agenda of certain conference organizers. What kind of response would I get afterward?

"Luis Palau's message is the only one that discussed evangelism like we practice it in Brazil," one delegate said afterward. "Evangelism must be evangelistic," said another, "just like Dr. Palau stressed in his message." That latter statement may seem redundant, but it's absolutely true! Out of the disillusionment of CLADE II, many expressed the desire for a new voice for Latin American Christians. That dream would come true a year later in Thailand, of all places.

The next month, it was back to real evangelism again. Our crusade in Caracas, Venezuela's oil-rich capital city, reached all levels of society, from President Dr. Luis Herrera Campins at the nation's first Presidential Prayer Breakfast, to the masses when I explained the Gospel on the nationwide *Frente a la Prensa* (Meet the Press) television news program.

In Caracas, I was surprised how many of the nation's most prestigious businessmen and government leaders were Christians. Never before had we received the active support of so many upper class citizens who were truly born-again. We even discovered the chief member of President Herrera's cabinet had been listening daily to our Spanish radio programs for a long time and couldn't have been more excited that we had come to the capital for a crusade. His enthusiastic greeting on the opening night of our meetings set the tone for the whole week.

Special affinity group events attracted 560 businessmen, military leaders, doctors, lawyers, and other professionals to a luncheon, and 700 middle and upper class women to an afternoon tea.

As in many other cities, attendance at our evening crusade meetings reflected the high percentage of young people in the nation (sixty-three percent under the age of twenty). The final two nights, the 13,500-seat El Poliedro sports arena was filled above capacity. All told, we saw more than 1,325 Venezuelans publicly respond when the invitation was given to receive Jesus Christ.

By now, the 1970s were drawing to a close. Had we accomplished our goal of saturating Latin America with the Gospel? In many ways, yes. We had ministered in many of the capitals and other leading cities across the continent. We had broadcast the Gospel via television and radio to at least one out of every three Spanish-speaking people in the world. We had distributed many millions of evangelistic booklets and tracts.

But the same doors that had been open for the Gospel the past decade had also remained open for the Marxists and other enemies of the Gospel. The battle for the heart and soul of Latin America was far from over!

What so greatly distressed me was how successful certain enemies of the Gospel had been in infiltrating and undermining the cause of Christ. We'd certainly seen that at CLADE II. And we'd seen it on other occasions, as well. Our team entered the 1980s more committed than ever to continue to evangelize the masses all across Latin America.

"Our God Reigns" tour

At the same time, it seemed the Lord was opening up even wider doors of opportunity in other parts of the world. We rang in the new decade with a fast-paced "Our God Reigns" evangelistic tour of England, sponsored by British Youth for Christ and *Buzz* magazine. We spoke at fifteen youth rallies in ten cities in two weeks, and 2,700 registered commitments to Jesus Christ. We gave numerous radio and newspaper interviews. Only a year earlier the BBC was calling Britain a "post-Christian" society. In private meetings with many young, emerging Christian leaders, such as Pete Meadows and Clive Calver, I challenged them to start thinking revival.

"God has no grandchildren," Welsh missionary David Morris had told me. He was right. A generation earlier, Britain was alive to God. Now, only one young person in 700 could answer basic Sunday school questions such as, "Who was Gideon?" Biblical illiteracy among youth was at its worst.

Not surprisingly, churches by the hundreds were closing, often being converted into mosques or Hindu temples. Every year, British companies were shipping hundreds of tons of obsolete, often ornate church furnishings to America, Japan, and Western Europe for auction to antique dealers.

Sadly, during the "Our God Reigns" tour, some of Britain's most prominent evangelicals were going on record stating there was nothing they could do to reverse such dismal trends. If it would take a third generation transplanted European who was born in the Third World and who now claimed American citizenship to help turn the tide in Britain, I decided, so be it.

29

That spring our team was back in Britain, this time for a six-city tour of Scotland. The biggest challenges we faced didn't come from the media, government officials, or anti-religious forces.

The *second* biggest challenge we faced came from within the church. People turned out for our evangelistic rallies and crusades by the droves. Two thousand committed their lives to Jesus Christ in a week and a half.

But behind closed doors, a dozen Scottish ministers met with me to voice their opposition to organized mass evangelistic efforts. To say I was shocked by our discussion may be a bit too strong. But I was quite surprised by the serious differences we had over some basic questions. At least half of the ministers were honest enough to say they did not accept the Bible as the trustworthy Word of God. Was it any wonder their churches were faltering and failing? Who wants to listen to ministers who readily dismiss portions of Scripture? Since when did God ask for anyone's help to make His Book more politically correct?

How different the attitude of those just coming to faith in Jesus Christ. One sixteen-year-old girl converted the previous June in Aberdeen wrote to tell us the past few months had been "the best of my whole life." The Lord had completely changed her life. She was growing to love God "more and more." She was reading the Bible regularly "and the more I read it the more I understand God's ways." She was praying, going to church regularly, preparing for her baptism, and witnessing to her family and friends. That story was now being repeated in thousands of people's lives throughout the nation.

Cancer

Just as we were leaving Scotland, however, Patricia and I suddenly found ourselves faced with the biggest challenge of our lives when she discovered a lump in one breast. We rushed home. Yes, there was a problem. A biopsy was necessary. Then came the doctor's verdict.

For a moment we sat in stunned silence, trying to block out his awful words. "The tumor is malignant and radical surgery must be performed immediately. We can't delay." Surgery was scheduled for the following Monday.

Pat had cancer.

When we got back to the house, I headed to my office in the basement. Somehow I had to come to grips with this terrible blow, I told myself. But a hundred emotions welled up inside me, and I began to weep. *This was the sort of thing that happens to other people, but not to my wife. Not to Pat.*

My thoughts were instantly interrupted by the strains of a familiar old hymn. Where was it coming from? Our four boys were all at school. No one was in the house except Pat and me.

Slowly it dawned on me—Pat herself was playing the piano and singing, "How Firm a Foundation." As the bottom was falling out of our lives, the Lord reminded us both how desperately we needed to base our security and strength in Him alone.

No one in this life is exempt from struggles, heartaches, and difficulties, of course. I'd known that since I was a boy. My own mother had been widowed at age thirty-five. That she was even able to keep our family together was a miracle. I was reminded, *God will see us through these deep waters, too.*

Deep waters they were. After I broke the news to our four boys, there was a long moment of silence. Then my youngest son, Steve, who was only eleven years old at the time, blurted out, "But, Daddy, people die from cancer!"

"That's true, but we believe God is going to make Mommy better again. She won't be feeling very well for a long time, so that will mean some changes around here, for all of us. You guys are going to have to not only learn to take care of yourselves, but also to help Mommy every way you can."

While Pat was recuperating at home after surgery, we carefully reviewed all our well-laid plans. Everything was up for grabs. For instance, should I go to Los Angeles for our first full-scale Spanish-language crusade here in America, or cancel the whole thing at the last minute?

Arrangements for that crusade had been two years in the making. The publicity was all out. Pat said I should go. Our two oldest sons, Kevin and Keith, now seventeen years old, could stay home to help take care of her. I could take the two younger boys with me. They were already used to the idea of traveling with Daddy from time to time, so it turned out to be a good decision, one which helped ease the turbulent feelings we all were experiencing. Yes, Mommy was sick. But we would take good care of her while she tried to get better.

Pat started chemotherapy treatment, at first every week, then every other week when she got too sick. We knew the current statistics of survival rates and all the rest. But we refused to play the "What if?" game. Pat's life was in God's hands. We also refused to give in to blasphemy. We dared not shake our fist in God's face, no matter what so-called experts said about "the need to vent your feelings." Third, we refused to second-guess the medical treatment she was receiving. Her doctor knew what he was doing.

You wouldn't believe the amount of free advice people dished out to us. I waylaid most of the least helpful articles and books that arrived in the mail to spare Pat the grief of tossing them herself. At one point I had to tell someone, "Look, lady, you can cut people's hair, but you are not going to give us medical advice!" That was the last thing Pat needed at that point.

What she did need and so appreciated were the calls and visits of friends who listened and shared an appropriate verse of Scripture with Pat. Jeremiah 29:11 became a favorite:

"I know the plans I have for you," declares the LORD, "plans to prosper you and not to harm you, plans to give you hope and a future."

When Andrew, Steve, and I got back from Los Angeles, Pat and I talked again about my schedule. This last crusade had been fruitful. Nearly 2,000 had committed their lives to the Lord, including a fourteen-year-old gang member who had just been treated at a hospital for gun-shot and knife wounds. I had met with Mayor Tom Bradley and received favorable coverage from *The Los Angeles Times* and other media.

But hard decisions had to be made. That included canceling a trip in June to the Congress on World Evangelization in Pattaya, Thailand, where I was scheduled to give a major address.

After our team's experience at CLADE II the previous year, we were eager to meet with other key Latin American Christian leaders and address the theological crisis of the moment. The Latin American Council of Churches would be in Pattaya, claiming to speak for all Christians in the region, even though their theological views contradicted the views of more than ninety percent of the continent's Protestants. Some observers even charged the LACC with seeking to infiltrate churches with so-called "liberation theology." Something must be done!

Thankfully, one of my key team members, Marcelino Ortiz, who headed up our team's regional office in Mexico City, stepped into the gap. He was appointed executive secretary of an ad hoc committee charged with the responsibility of calling a Consultation of Evangelicals in Latin America (CONELA) by early 1982. Another team member, Bill Conard, also was appointed to serve on the ad hoc committee, and I was asked to serve on the advisory board.

There was no doubt that leftist ideologies were penetrating the Latin church. The question of the hour was, *Could CONELA provide a united defense of the Gospel and take the offensive in showing how to apply biblical principles to the issues of life?*

Within two years, the answer would be a resounding "Yes!"

Guayaquil '80

News of the ad hoc CONELA committee was received enthusiastically wherever we went that fall, including five cities in South America's southern cone and Guayaquil, Ecuador, where we repeated our *Continente '75* strategy on a regional basis with great success. My *Guayaquil '80* crusade messages were broadcast by HCJB Radio to at least ten nations. We even received a cable from Havana, Cuba, telling us, "Every night we listen to *Guayaquil '80*. May the Lord bless you."

After each evening crusade meeting, I rushed to a local television studio to do our live call-in counseling program that was broadcast for twelve consecutive nights, via twenty-five repeater stations, to the entire nation and to much of neighboring Colombia and Peru, as well.

While more than 2,800 came forward during the Guayaquil crusade meetings, only in eternity will we know how many truly came to Christ through the simultaneous media outreach. But we do know 180 people called to complain when the nightly radio broadcasts stopped, unheard of for almost any other kind of programming!

I started thinking, *With Pat so sick, why not make more extensive use of the media this next year?* My team members readily agreed. With

Central America reeling from recent guerrilla attacks and civil war, the region seemed a natural target for an all-out evangelistic media blitz.

We decided to concentrate on Guatemala, where we had already seen so much fruit and where we had been invited to return in two years for the centennial celebration of the Gospel's coming to that nation.

Worry about oldest sons

Besides Pat's battle with cancer, there were other reasons to consider curtailing my crusade travels. Our two oldest sons were definitely becoming enthralled with the world. Pat told me bluntly, "If you don't stay home, these boys will go straight into the world." I panicked. To think of any of our sons walking away from the Lord broke my heart.

Pat and I agreed if we saw no change in Kevin and Keith over the next six months, I would drop all of my crusade commitments and stay home to be with them. It was a desperate decision, but one we felt we had to make.

Soon after that, Christian singer Keith Green came to town. The Lord used his deeply moving concert and a retreat our sons attended to revolutionize their lives. They consecrated their lives to God and applied to attend Wheaton College, an outstanding Christian school. Pat and I breathed a sigh of relief. *Thank You, Lord. We can carry on.* Not that our struggles were over, by any means.

30

Because of Pat's ongoing battle with cancer and grueling chemotherapy treatments, I kept my travel schedule to a minimum in 1981—only two crusades. To be honest, I wish I'd done only one, and a shorter one, at that.

Pat was in full agreement that I should go to Glasgow, Scotland, for the culmination of our three-year strategy to help re-evangelize that nation. You can't make a national impact overnight, but five weeks in the capital was almost too long.

"It's either back to the Bible or back to the jungle," I mentioned on the opening Sunday of our Glasgow crusade, echoing something Billy Graham had said once.

Journalists couldn't resist the temptation. The following morning the remark appeared on the front page of the *Glasgow Herald*. It became the topic of discussion and, at times, heated debate on television, radio, and the editorial pages of several newspapers for days.

I used the controversy to remind audiences that at one time the city's motto was, "Let Glasgow flourish by the preaching of the Word and the praising of His Name." Now it was simply, "Let Glasgow flourish." While that abbreviated motto may have suggested the sincere will and aspirations of the city's current planners, the facts suggested just the opposite. Well-known corporations, including Rolls Royce, had left the city. Unemployment was at seventeen percent and climbing. Less than four percent of the population regularly attended church. Dozens of church buildings had been closed in the past year.

Friendship evangelists

Our team trained hundreds of friendship evangelists, committed Christians who agreed to regularly pray by name for five or ten family members and neighbors, work associates, and friends who had not yet received Jesus Christ as Savior. We then challenged them to invite one and all to the Kelvin Hall crusade meetings.

One teenage girl, who lived about fifteen miles from Kelvin Hall, rented a bus, convinced she could fill it with friends. What initiative! But when she invited her friends, not one accepted. She was so shaken she called the crusade prayer committee and asked them to intercede. Then she went back to her friends and persuaded thirty-eight of them to attend the crusade with her. At Kelvin Hall, all thirty-eight went forward to give their lives to Christ!

Many other friendship evangelists reported seeing three, five, even ten people they knew come to Christ during the crusade. All told, more than 5,325 publicly gave their lives to the Lord during the thirty-six day crusade.

Was it worth the long haul, day in and day out, slugging it out for five straight weeks? Definitely. From the thousands of new converts, God began raising up a new generation of Scottish pastors, teachers, missionaries, and at least one itinerant evangelist, Richard Gibbons, whom I had the privilege of meeting several years later. Evangelism was back on the map in Scotland.

Could the same thing happen in England? Privately, Billy Graham had told me he didn't think he'd ever go back there again for another crusade. The spiritual revival he'd seen during the 1950s was all but gone. If Scotland had been spiritually dying, England was quite nearly dead. Still, our team accepted invitations for crusades in the cities of Leeds and London, capital of the once great British Commonwealth. Even Billy changed his mind later and agreed to help re-evangelize the land.

First American crusade

But what about America? Ever since coming to this country, I had felt God telling me I should pour myself into crusade evangelism overseas until Billy Graham started slowing down. Twenty years had come and gone. Billy was still going as strong as ever. I began to wonder if I'd ever get my chance. *Was my dream of evangelizing America's cities always going to be only a dream?*

With some hesitation, I accepted an invitation for our team to go to San Diego for our first full-scale English-language American crusade during August of 1981. Afterward, I regretted the decision. Not that Pat was concerned about my leaving for a week and a half. Not that we weren't well received in San Diego. And not that we didn't see a great response to the Gospel, with more than 1,200 committing their lives to Jesus Christ. But I felt I'd somehow disobeyed the Lord. Yes, God *was* opening the door for us to expand our ministry in the United States, but it would open slowly, according to His schedule, not mine.

It was delightful to have Pat join me in San Diego. She spoke one morning to a group of 2,000 women about her struggles with cancer and the need to trust Jesus Christ to stand strong through life's storms. I didn't keep it a secret how much I admired her strength and endurance the past fourteen months despite repeated periods of weariness, sickness, discomfort, and pain.

Kevin and Keith flew out of the nest that fall, for their first semester at Wheaton College. They returned home for the holidays a few days after a bone scan revealed Pat had no signs of cancer anywhere. We celebrated Christmas and New Year's in a big way! We were all back together again. And for the moment, at least, Pat's cancer was gone.

As a family, we thanked the Lord for sparing Pat's life. In my heart, I also thanked God for using that time of adversity to give Pat a wider platform for ministry. Suddenly, editors were asking *her* for articles. She started receiving many more invitations to speak at women's conferences and evangelistic meetings. Crusade committees wanted her to come and share her testimony, as well. With our four sons getting older, the timing couldn't have been better.

If 1981 was a relatively quiet year, 1982 started with a bang with seven crusades scheduled on four continents. First stop was the University of Wisconsin in Madison that February. I couldn't believe how open the campus was to spiritual issues. Yet I was astounded to learn that most of the Christian student leaders—from groups such as Campus Crusade for Christ, Inter-Varsity Christian Fellowship, The Navigators, plus Lutheran Campus Center, Baptist Student Union, and Black Campus Ministry—came from broken homes or homes where the parents were unconverted.

One night I remarked, "There was a time when parents prayed for their children. Now children pray for their parents."

After the meeting a man came up to me smelling of alcohol and said, "Luis, I am one of those parents being prayed for by my children." More than ever I was convinced, *Surely we need to re-evangelize this land!*

From Wisconsin it was on to Newcastle, Australia; then Bellingham, Washington; Helsinki, Finland; Asunción, Paraguay; Leeds, England; and Guatemala City. Not since 1969 had we attempted so many crusades in such a short period of time.

Pat completed her grueling chemotherapy program just in time to join me for the closing week of the Newcastle crusade. It was great to have been invited to return for a second crusade, following up on what we'd started three years earlier. Through the crusade meetings, media interviews, and live television counseling, the city opened up to the Gospel in an amazing way. If it were humanly possible, I'd love to go back to every city where we've had a crusade. We often see two, three, even four times as much fruit.

In Bellingham, in the picturesque northwest corner of the continental United States, we saw a touch of revival, even though it's one of the least churched regions in the nation. God worked in a wonderful way, convicting men, women, and young people and turning many to Himself.

Response to scandals

That same month, I was deeply grieved to learn that a respected youth evangelist with whom we had worked in the past had left his wife, his children, and his ministry for the passions of the flesh. It turned out that secretly, for years, he had been feeding a pornography addiction while preaching up a storm against immorality. Then, the inevitable happened. He started committing adultery. He had affairs going in city after city. Finally, the truth came out, and he walked out on his family.

I couldn't believe the news, yet I could. At a Christian conference we both attended a few months earlier, this youth evangelist had told me, "Luis, you may hear one of these days about a teenage girl who goes around saying I had a love affair with her. Don't believe a word of it." But when I pressed him to tell me the truth about the matter, he grew very cold and said, "Forget it, I wish I hadn't mentioned it." He protested his innocence, but I wondered.

When the truth came out, it shook our whole team. The Lord had kept us from dishonoring His name all these years. I prayed, *Lord, please keep us till the end of the road, faithful, holy, fruitful for Your glory.*

I later tried to win this fallen brother back to God, to no avail. He was sorry for all the sorrow he had heaped upon himself, all right, yet he refused to repent of his wicked ways and get back to God. He did try to get back into the ministry as if nothing had happened, but he was finished. You can't play games with God like that.

During this period, a rash of other influential servants of God fell into rather despicable sins. It's happened before and would happen again. Church history makes that clear. But at the time it seems like an epidemic. You wonder, *What's going on? If this could happen to so-and-so, and so-and-so, and so-and-so, it could happen to me.*

I talked to Dick Hillis about this. "Why are all these guys falling away?"

Dick thought and thought about it. After walking with the Lord for sixty-some years, he's no fly-by-night. Finally, he told me, "I think it's because they were reading a lot of books about the Bible, but not the Bible itself." The more I thought about it, the more I could see his point. Nothing can take the place of God's Word, not even the best biblical commentaries. Sure, an evangelist or preacher or teacher needs to do his homework. He needs to read widely and deeply. But even Billy Graham himself once admitted if he could do it all over again, he would have read fewer books and spent even more time reading The Book. Saturating myself with Scripture would be my goal, too.

31

I f I was serious about staying in God's Word before, I was all the more determined after talking to Dick Hillis. Sure, I knew many evangelistic passages by heart. I could quote them word for word in English and Spanish. I'd been studying the Scriptures daily all my adult life. But that was no excuse to slack off now!

The next month, May 1982, we were off to Helsinki, capital of Finland, where the state and free churches came together for the first united evangelistic crusade in that country since the Reformation. That fact did not go unnoticed by the media, which deluged us with requests for interviews.

It was also our first full-fledged crusade outside the English- and Spanish-speaking worlds. I'd had people translate for me before, but never all day long, all week long, for every single event. I couldn't even ask a waitress for a cup of coffee without someone else's help. It was a humbling experience, especially when I saw how the Holy Spirit so intricately wove my words with my translator's as we proclaimed the Gospel in one language and then another. Because I'd often translated for others in the past, I knew some common mistakes to avoid, which definitely helped.

Then it was back to Paraguay, where we'd had a glorious crusade in the capital, Asunción, six years earlier. This time, we were working with a team of associate evangelists, convinced God would open up the entire nation to the Gospel through us. And He did! On the opening Sunday, we set a team record for the most people counseled in a single meeting. Revival was in the air!

Then, on the closing Sunday, we saw the Lord break that brand-new record when an astounding 1,690 people came forward to give their lives to the Lord. All told, more than 10,550 people registered public commitments to Christ. Churches doubled in size overnight. Only in Bolivia had we ever seen a larger number turn to Christ in less than three weeks.

In every way, the devil was defeated in Paraguay. His strategies failed miserably. We felt no spiritual resistance to the proclamation of the Gospel.

Spiritual warfare in England

We found exactly the opposite to be true in Leeds, England, a few weeks later. I'd never seen such spiritual warfare in all my life. The youth of England might have been biblically illiterate, but they were quite knowledgeable when it came to the occult. During four of the nightly meetings, members of a Satanic group openly ridiculed us, heckling whenever I read from the Bible or mentioned the blood of Jesus Christ.

On one occasion, several of the occultists actually rushed past security guards and stormed the platform as I read from Ephesians 6. Another time, a deranged young woman who claimed to be "god" tried to grab the microphone next to me. Cult groups even were threatening to burn down the big-top tent where we held the crusade meetings.

The atmosphere was incredibly tense at every meeting. It was an all-out battle for the souls of men and women, youth and children, but the Lord gave us the victory, drawing nearly 1,000 to Himself.

One outstanding Christian leader, who witnessed the Satanic attacks, said, "Luis, you can expect more of the same and in greater variety and number when you go to London."

I swallowed hard. We were gearing up for more than 100 crusade meetings in London over the course of three months. I wondered, *Are we ready, come what may?*

Thankfully, the churches in Leeds took seriously their responsibility to care for all those who had just given their lives to the Lord. A few months later, research showed that seventy-nine percent of the decision-makers had been spiritually nurtured and were active in a local church. Of the university students who accepted Christ, the figure reported by the local clergy and chaplains was one hundred percent!

Massive revival in Guatemala

From de-christianized England it was back to Portland again briefly, then down to Guatemala for a crusade held in conjunction with the centennial celebration of the Gospel coming to the nation. Only a few months earlier, we wondered if we would have to cancel the plans. Then, after months of political upheaval, Guatemala finally began enjoying a period of relative peace. Our Central American field director, Benjamín Orozco, assured me the crusade could proceed as planned without incident. He was almost right.

The weeklong crusade received more media attention than any of our previous 175 crusades and rallies. Fifteen radio stations broadcast the messages live each night, including one station across the border in El Salvador. Two television stations aired more than twenty evangelistic messages I had taped.

Then early in the morning on Thanksgiving Sunday 1982, the entire nation held its breath as Christians from all across the nation prepared to celebrate 100 years of Gospel proclamation in that land in a big way.

Until then, no one knew for sure how many committed Christians there were in Guatemala. For years, I'd felt the Lord saying it would be the first nation to become fifty-one percent born-again. But nothing could have prepared us for what we saw that morning.

The day before, Christians from other parts of the country began flooding into the capital. Many stayed overnight with fellow believers living there in Guatemala City. Then, after sunrise, they all began marching in columns down the city's widest avenues toward Campo Marte, a massive empty military parade ground. Tens of thousands, then soon hundreds of thousands of people began filling the park. Military helicopters flew overhead, trying to get some estimate of the size of the crowd . . . first 500,000, then 600,000, finally 700,000 people! Afterward, historian Virgil Zapata called it the largest gathering of born-again Christians in the history not only of Guatemala, but also of all Latin America.

Fortunately, we had more than a dozen radio stations broadcasting my message live that day. Otherwise there would have been no way to synchronize the singing, let alone speak to such a vast sea of people. Trying to ask people to come forward was all but impossible. We'd have to leave the results in God's hands. Besides—unlike a regular crusade meeting where we like to see an evenly mixed audience of believers and unbelievers—this was mostly a time of celebration. And what a celebration it was!

It seemed the whole world sat up and finally began to take notice of what had been happening slowly but surely all across Latin America the past half-generation. Many wondered aloud, "If nearly three-quarters of á million born-again Christians gathered a few days ago for a single meeting in Guatemala City, how many others might there be throughout the continent?"

Tens of millions!

Much has been said through the years about the importance of one-on-one evangelism. I agree, it is crucial. After all, the Lord said we would be His witnesses. But Jesus demonstrated the wisdom and necessity of preaching to the masses, and commissioned His disciples to reach the nations. And reach the peoples of the world they did, from the day of Pentecost on.

Even though the effectiveness of mass evangelism is clear from Scripture, church history, and experience, it is not without its critics. Within the church, a small handful of lesser known but vocal church growth "experts" argue against the methodology, often repeating outdated statistics (from a 1976 Billy Graham Seattle crusade, for instance) that have long since been refuted.

Other critics have severely criticized Billy Graham and myself for meeting with presidents, prime ministers, and other top government officials, as if they didn't need Christ, too! Even to this day, I'm still criticized, especially whenever I go to Western Europe, for meeting with Guatemala's President Jose Efrain Rios Montt in 1982, with Paraguay's President Alfredo Stroessner six years earlier, and with other so-called "right-wing dictators" at Presidential Prayer Breakfasts and private meetings. Supposedly, I should be more politically correct. What's ironic is I've *never* been criticized for meeting with "left-wing" dictators in Eastern Europe. But you can't have it both ways!

> The Lord is not slack concerning His promise, as some count slackness, but is longsuffering toward us, not willing that *any* should perish but that *all* should come to repentance (2 Peter 3:9 NKJV, *emphasis mine*).

A few weeks later, together with other leaders, I shared the platform with President Ronald Reagan at the National Religious Broadcasters (NRB) convention in Washington, D.C. Journalists often ask if I'm Republican or Democrat. I reply I'm for evangelizing both! It's all too easy for people to claim God is on their side politically. Nothing could be further from the truth. The Lord of hosts never comes to take sides; He comes to take over! (Joshua 5:13–6:5).

After preaching to 700,000 people in Guatemala City, some openly wondered why we still had smaller crusades on my schedule. Why, for instance, were we going next to the city of Hermosillo, Mexico, where evangelicals made up less than one percent of the population and the crusade venue (a gymnasium) held a maximum of 5,000 people per night? Simply because, after much prayer, we felt the leading of the Holy Spirit to accept an invitation from that city's Christian leaders to come for a crusade.

Admittedly, sometimes our team's choices defy natural logic. But we saw the Lord work miracles in Hermosillo beyond all expectation. First, we were able to run nearly 350 radio spots and thirty television announcements on local stations, breaking the stronghold of long-standing government prohibitions against religious broadcasting. Second, Marxists loudly and publicly criticized us, generating additional publicity and interest in the proclamation of the Gospel at our crusade meetings, free of charge! Third, the gymnasium was filled to overflowing each night, with latecomers listening to the service over loudspeakers installed outside the building.

Most important, 3,450 people (including the city's mayor) received Jesus Christ or rededicated their lives to the Lord. The born-again population of Hermosillo doubled in a week!

In my opinion, it's futile to even ask, *Shouldn't we wait to accept only the biggest and best possible crusade invitations?* That's absurd. Our team's conviction is that we must make the most of every year the Lord gives us.

When our lives are over, what will really count is, Were we faithful to the Great Commission? Or will we confront people at the judgment seat of Christ who will say, "I lived in such-and-such a place and no man cared for my soul"?

32

Rarely has our team lacked for crusade invitations. We were deluged with requests, however, after speaking to 4,000 delegates from 133 nations during Amsterdam '83, the first International Conference of Itinerant Evangelists sponsored by the Billy Graham Evangelistic Association.

Billy Graham spoke on the opening night of the ten-day conference. The next evening, he asked me to speak on the sensitive subject of personal holiness. When I finished speaking, everyone in the audience got down on his knees on the convention floor, at Cliff Barrows's suggestion, and prayed in his own language, appealing to God for His cleansing power to make each one a mighty force for evangelism around the world. Many wept. The effect was profound.

Ten days later, in his closing message, Billy shared from his heart: "This year, I will be sixty-five. At best, I don't have left more than a few years of this intensive evangelism that we engage in. Physically, it would be impossible. I have been engaged in it now over forty years. Three-fourths of my time is gone. At seventy-five I may still be able to hold some crusades, of course, but not on the scale we are doing now."

Here in the U.S. and abroad, journalists were asking, "Who is going to fill Billy's shoes once he's gone?" They're still wondering, more than a decade later. But the answer should be rather obvious: *no one man.*

That next month our team traveled to Modesto, California, the home of Cliff Barrows's family and site of one of Billy Graham's earliest citywide crusades back in late 1948. The unity we witnessed among approximately 130 churches representing twenty-six denominations was amazing. Together, they supplied an army of more than 2,500 volunteers to assist with the crusade meetings and follow-up efforts. Choir members, ushers, and counselors alike rejoiced with us when overflow crowds filled the Modesto Junior College stadium all week and more than 1,400 inquirers came forward to publicly register their decision for Christ.

It was thrilling to have such a successful crusade in Modesto, but in many ways little had changed. The primary focus of our ministry was still overseas. We had now had three crusades in America over the past three years and would have five more over the next five years. It wouldn't be until 1989 that I felt God had given us the green light to rapidly accelerate our ministries by holding several American crusades each year and making greater use of the media in this country.

Mission to London

Overseas, the green lights couldn't have been flashing brighter. We blanketed London with nine regional crusades that fall of 1983, setting the stage for an even more ambitious seven-week crusade in a central location six months later.

The BBC was so intrigued they decided to make the crusade—particularly the content of the Gospel message I was preaching—the subject of an hour-long documentary. They assigned one of their top producers to the project. The hard-hitting documentary aired on New Year's Day 1984, reaching millions of people watching television. The incredible thing was, it was impossible to buy time to broadcast the Gospel in England in those days. But the Good News came through loud and clear, and we have reason to believe many individuals and families were converted while watching BBC that evening (and the next two New Year's Days, as well).

Six weeks later, two half-hour segments I did with Dr. James Dobson were broadcast nationwide on his popular *Focus on the Family* radio program. Dr. Dobson asked me about our crusades in Latin America and Britain, then asked me to explain how the Gospel applies to men, women, and young people. It was the first time, someone on his staff told me, that Dr. Dobson had ever asked a guest to lead listeners in a prayer of salvation. To see him in tears moved me profoundly. Afterward, thousands of people requested a copy of the program. You can imagine my surprise ten years later when, at the last minute, I was invited to share the National Religious Broadcasters annual convention platform with Dr. Dobson and Rep. James Talent, a freshman congressman from Missouri, who told how he heard that February 1984 broadcast, pulled off the highway, bowed his head, and prayed with us to receive Christ!

Scores of moving testimonies could be told from both phases of our Mission to London, which concluded with six non-stop weeks of preaching, night after night, in Queen's Park Rangers (QPR) Stadium. People of every creed, color, religious background, and walk of life trusted Jesus Christ—a member of the royal family, a top rock star, a famous actress, a disillusioned policeman, a car dealer, a truck driver, a bus driver interviewed that same night by BBC Radio, at least one member of the BBC staff, the official crusade photographer, an Australian soccer player, a young businesswoman, a gentleman whose wife had prayed for his salvation for twenty-one years, twenty-five boys at a British boarding school, a young gang member who had helped disrupt the meeting earlier that same evening, a runaway teenager, and more than a few religious ministers. What a dream come true!

During the crusade, one of my team members talked with a man on the street who had just helped a drunk escape being run over by traffic. The man mentioned that he had been an alcoholic himself and had been taken for dead and rushed to a local hospital only three weeks earlier. A few days later he went forward at QPR Stadium to accept Jesus Christ as Savior. Gloriously converted and completely freed from alcohol, he even began singing in the crusade choir!

By the final night, cumulative attendance for Mission to London had topped 518,000 and more than 28,000 had made public commitments to Jesus Christ. To God alone be all the glory!

With Billy Graham simultaneously holding crusades in other parts of England, the nation was shaken by the Gospel. What's more, the last week of June my messages were broadcast to the entire British Commonwealth—fifty nations, all told.

"Congratulations on superlative Christian radio at its finest," wrote one Grenadian government official. "The world needs more of this. You have created a demand for more. What now?" I was glad to be able to say we already had similar media outreaches in the works to reach both Latin American (1985) and Asia (1986) with the Good News of salvation in Jesus' name.

All told, the crusade cost two million pounds. That certainly caught the media's attention. In press conferences and interviews, however, I made no apologies. It's preventive medicine to help correct the ills of society, an investment in lives for all eternity. Given the billions of dollars spent every year on our children's education, and other tens of billions spent on summer vacations and other forms of entertainment, what's a few hundred thousand dollars to win thousands of lives and souls to Jesus Christ?

The sheer length and breadth of the crusade staggered the press. They reported on every possible angle, including "Luis go home!" graffiti that began appearing around the city. I would have gone home sooner if the crusade hadn't been such an overwhelming success that the local committee extended it two extra weeks.

To me, success is doing what pleases God. From Scripture, it's clear that nothing pleases the Father more than when a man, woman, or child is "rescued . . . from the domain of darkness and brought . . . into the kingdom of the Son he loves, in whom we have redemption, the forgiveness of sins" (Colossians 1:13-14).

In the Gospels, Jesus says there's rejoicing in heaven when even one person repents (Luke 15). What a celebration there must be when thousands turn to the Lord during a crusade!

Critics will say, "But it isn't decisions that count, it's disciples." Yes, the Lord commanded us to "make disciples of all nations" (Matthew 28:19). But you can't make disciples if no one makes a decision to actually receive Jesus Christ.

Successful follow-up

Thankfully, the London crusade committee and many churches took their responsibility to care for new believers seriously. MARC Europe conducted an in-depth church growth research study afterward and discovered that nearly eighty percent of all adult decision-makers were active in local churches and going on for the Lord six months later. The implications were astounding, refuting oft-repeated accusations that crusade evangelism somehow doesn't produce lasting results, which is utter nonsense.

Church growth researchers have conducted major studies after several of our crusades over the years. Their findings have been published here and abroad. The facts speak for themselves. In the parable of the soils, Jesus made it clear that not all converts go on to bear fruit. But a clear majority of crusade converts do!

I love it every time I meet or hear from a crusade convert who is on fire for the Lord and who has led a host of other people to the Lord. Often, whole families turn to God through the witness of one crusade decision-maker. One such convert wrote to tell me: "Mission to London is not over, not by a long way. The QPR statistics will show that 'x' number of people gave their lives to Jesus on June 15th, 1984, but multiply that figure by five and it will be more accurate."

Another time, a lady led a group of six people up to me after a meeting and said, "Luis, I was converted at last summer's crusade." Her eyes sparkled as she added, "And since then all six of these people have received Christ into their hearts—my husband over there, his sister, my two daughters, my fourteen-year-old son, and my best friend. May we have our picture taken with you?" That's the kind of human drama that moves me to keep on preaching Jesus until I meet Him face to face someday.

Do I have any regrets about Mission to London? I wish we could have gone on another six weeks. My only other disappointment was that, after all those months, I was still unable to convince some ministers that their congregations would be blessed by God if only they would wholeheartedly get involved in the crusade. That certain churches participated in name only grieved my heart.

Our team's own post-crusade research has shown that if a church is actively involved in one of our crusades, it will receive seven times more growth afterward than a church that holds back and doesn't train its people to be friendship evangelists, counselors, and follow-up workers.

Shining Path on the rampage

That fall, our team was invited back to Peru, where Maoist *Sendero Luminoso* (Shining Path) guerrillas had pushed the nation to the brink of anarchy, wiping out whole villages, executing military and civil authorities, and martyring Christian leaders as well in their attempt to create a "new society." More than forty pastors and 400 other believers had been killed in the bloody wake of the Shining Path.

Then came news that the Shining Path guerrillas had become even more violent, invading the United Press International offices in Lima, blowing up an American owned department store, even attacking the American Embassy. It was all-out war.

As an American evangelist, would I still risk coming for two and one-half weeks of out-and-out evangelism in two of Peru's largest cities?

Yes, come what may.

33

It's impossible to call a nation to Jesus Christ and try to escape the notice of the enemies of the Gospel. You can do one or the other, but not both.

There was cause for great rejoicing when our first crusade, in the city of Arequipa, Peru, concluded without incident. Some 9,000 people packed the city's indoor coliseum for the last meeting, and 2,317 of them—a full twenty-five percent—made public commitments to Jesus Christ that night. That figure was the highest single-meeting response rate we'd seen in two decades of ministry!

But the Shining Path guerrillas were ready for us that night. The next morning we were to fly to Lima, Peru's capital. They sent a messenger to warn me to get out of Peru immediately or die "a painful dog's death." I wasn't sure what that meant, but I wasn't anxious to find out.

Before God, I determined we couldn't quit now and go home with our tail between our legs. "Knowing the fear of the Lord, we persuade men" (2 Corinthians 5:11, RSV). *We must press on!*

When our crusade meetings at Lima's Alianza Stadium proceeded as planned, the terrorists tried to shut us down by destroying Lima's electrical power plants. More than 30,000 people gasped when the stadium lights flickered after a series of explosions.

If we lose power, I realized, scores of people could lose their lives or be severely hurt in the ensuing pandemonium.

Lima disappeared. In an instant, the entire city lost its electrical power, almost everywhere except—miraculously—the neighborhood surrounding the Alianza Stadium. I breathed deeply, then continued preaching with an extra sense of urgency and desire to see thousands more trust Christ, before it was too late.

For obvious reasons, we rescheduled the last two nights of the crusade as afternoon meetings. Security measures were the tightest in our team's history. Nevertheless, on the closing day of the crusade, even though we'd changed the time of the meeting, 40,000 people packed the stadium and more than 3,000 people committed their lives to Christ—setting another record for the largest number ever to come forward in any of our meetings, anywhere.

Occasionally our team is accused of talking about numbers too much. In many parts of the world, however, people are being born by the thousands and dying by the thousands, but being won to Christ by ones and twos. Our desire is to reach the masses, exclusively giving God all the honor and glory for the numbers of people who commit their lives to Him.

While we were in the capital, I had an hour-long meeting with Peruvian President Fernando Belaunde Terry. We prayed together for God's peace on the nation, and later I was allowed to pray again on nationwide television.

Our team also finally had an opportunity to meet Rosario Rivera, the well-known Peruvian communist guerrilla who came to Christ during our last crusade in Peru almost fifteen years earlier and who was now boldly speaking out for the Christian faith. Once an associate of Che Guevara, Rosario now led a small army of Christians engaged in large-scale evangelism and relief work in the city's worst slums. She's still at it today. What a marvelous example of the transforming power of the Gospel!

The success of our crusades in Peru added momentum to *Continente '85*. During Easter Holy Week, we blanketed the Spanish-speaking world with evangelistic broadcasts on more than 330 radio and 480 television stations—five times more stations than our *Continente '75* network a decade earlier.

The next month Vice President and presidential candidate George Bush spoke to undergraduate students and I spoke to graduate students at Wheaton College's commencement, which was a special privilege since my sons Kevin and Keith were graduating with honors that day.

Challenges in Switzerland

Two weeks later, I spoke in quite a different setting. Toward the beginning of a three-week crusade in Zurich, the Swiss Evangelical Alliance invited me to speak at a special Ascension Day service in Geneva. When they realized how large a crowd probably would attend, they asked for permission to meet in the chapel room at the headquarters of the World Council of Churches. Dr. Emilio Castro, WCC general secretary, welcomed us when we arrived. I didn't know what to think. I'd preached the Gospel in a lot of different settings to a lot of different audiences, but nothing like this.

Some in the audience openly opposed everything for which I stood and later said so. But I was the guest speaker that day. The message was a clear statement of the biblical teaching on Jesus Christ's death, resurrection, ascension, and second coming, with particular emphasis on the social impact of preaching the Gospel to all nations and inviting individuals to place their trust in Christ.

Some misunderstood why I'd agreed to preach at WCC headquarters. Several at WCC headquarters weren't too happy with me, either. A while later someone apparently in attendance that day mailed out six single-spaced pages of blatant lies about me, causing untold grief.

D. L. Moody was certainly right. "A lie will travel around the world," he once said, "while truth is still putting on its boots." Be that as it may, our reputation remains in God's hands. He always vindicates us in the end.

Back in Zurich, I reminded Swiss journalists about their nation's rich Reformation heritage 450 years ago, then told them, "I believe a new wave of mass evangelism is about to hit Europe. A new Reformation is needed on this continent." It was the first time in memory that both secular and religious journalists jointly had attended a press conference in that city. A remarkable forty-five publications, seven radio stations, and two television stations reported on the crusade.

While the media coverage was extraordinary, the crusade meetings themselves were every bit as tough as we'd expected them to be. Trying to do mass evangelism in Western Europe is like pulling teeth. Still, cumulative crusade attendance topped 112,000 and more than 1,230 people registered public commitments to Jesus Christ. Nearly 1,600 more gave their lives to Christ during evangelistic rallies in Denmark, England, France, The Netherlands, and Norway.

The very end of that summer, September 19 and 20, a series of terrifying earthquakes devastated Mexico City, killing thousands and leaving thousands more injured and homeless. The regional offices for LPEA and CONELA were located in one of the business districts hardest hit by the quakes. Due to severe structural damage, the offices had to be demolished. In the rubble of the worst natural disaster in the nation's 500-year history, our Mexico City team members and CONELA colleagues faced the overwhelming task of starting over almost from scratch.

I immediately sent our vice president of Spanish ministries, Jim Williams, to assess the situation. I flew down a short while later. We'd both served as full-time missionaries in Mexico City and lived there with our families only a few years earlier. We shuddered at the sight of such a terrible disaster. Instinctively, we set up an emergency relief fund to send tens of thousands of dollars of financial aid. In conjunction with that relief effort, we saw hundreds receive Christ.

Revival in Argentina

The next spring, I returned to the homeland of my birth, Argentina, for a three-week national crusade. An estimated 80,000 attended our opening rally in Buenos Aires on Easter Sunday. Hundreds of thousands more flocked to our other crusade meetings throughout Argentina. After years of slow but steady spiritual growth, the revival I'd always dreamed of seeing was unleashed with more than 12,300 coming forward to commit their lives to Jesus Christ.

Other thousands were reached by our six live call-in television broadcasts, which drew an estimated total audience of 18 million viewers—the largest audience for any midnight television program in Argentina's history. One woman called, verbally insulted me in front of millions of other viewers, then abruptly hung up. On the air, I invited her to come to the Velez Sarsfield soccer stadium to hear the Gospel. She came the next night, cried throughout the message, and turned her life over to the Lord when I gave the invitation.

Another woman called up two minutes before we went off the air that night. Ever since her father had been killed two years earlier, she had been severely depressed and had already tried to take her life three times. She was desperate. I counseled her for fifteen minutes after the program ended, then invited her to meet the next day with team member Jim Williams, who has his doctorate in biblical counseling. The next day she came to our crusade counseling center, heard the Gospel, and committed her life to Christ. Immediately, her whole outlook on life changed. Suddenly, she had a reason for living!

Granted, Argentinians love to stay up late, but we were dumbfounded when hundreds of viewers kept calling in for hours after we went off the air. People were absolutely desperate to hear how Christ could change their lives. Biblical counselors trained by Dr. Williams were still leading callers to Christ all day long and halfway through the night a week later!

34

After returning home from Argentina, where we'd seen such an incredible revival of biblical Christianity, I poured myself into final preparations for our first Asian crusade, in Singapore, two months later.

Trying to understand the Chinese mentality is no easy task for a Western-trained person. I attended Chinese conferences, interviewed Chinese Christian leaders, and then thoroughly studied the books they had recommended. Because of the concern of the Chinese not to offend others, I realized it would be almost impossible to convince Singapore's foremost and most gracious Christian leaders to point out any cultural mistakes I might make while a guest in their country.

Beyond the tropical city-state of Singapore, our team also dreamed of reaching all of Asia with the Gospel. Through an historic partnership with Far East Broadcasting Company, Trans World Radio, HCJB, and many other missionary radio and television ministries, five of the Singapore National Stadium crusade messages were simultaneously translated into eight major Asian languages and broadcast throughout the continent via a radio and video network. Hundreds of thousands of copies of the evangelistic booklet *What Is a Real Christian?* were published, as well. All told, some 300 distributors in sixty nations helped us reach millions of Asians with the Gospel. The magnitude of this *Asia '86* outreach reached historic proportions. Never before had so many ministries worked hand in hand to reach so many Asian people in one fell swoop. What a divinely given, glorious privilege for a South American-born follower of Jesus Christ.

In Singapore itself, more than one-third of a million people attended the National Stadium crusade meetings, and 11,902 people publicly gave their lives to the Lord Jesus Christ. Other untold thousands were won to Christ in dozens of other nations, including the People's Republic of China. Invitations began pouring in for crusades in Hong Kong, India, Indonesia, Japan, the Philippines, Thailand, and other Asian nations. Another whole sphere of ministry was opening up to us and we loved it.

Later that month, my youngest son, Steve, accompanied me when I spoke at *Creation '86*, the largest outdoor Christian music festival in the world. Featured speakers included Josh McDowell, Melody Green, Juan Carlos Ortiz (my sister Martha's husband), and Tony Campolo. At Dr. Campolo's urging, Steve decided to sponsor a needy Mexican child through Compassion International—the best child sponsorship agency my wife, Pat, and I had ever seen.

Because of my experiences growing up and our family's two missionary terms overseas, we had always made it a priority to sponsor needy children. But never before had we seen an agency so committed to evangelism and discipleship, together with education and the medical needs of children, working through local churches.

On our own, we started talking up Compassion's ministry as one of the best ways to "raise tenderhearted children in a tough world," to quote a catchy phrase Pat coined. When one of her articles on the subject appeared in *Focus on the Family* magazine a couple of years later, Compassion International wrote to say thanks and ask if we would officially endorse their ministry. We'd already personally checked out their work overseas and knew it was outstanding, so we were glad to say yes.

A month later, I was asked to give one of the plenary addresses at the second International Conference for Itinerant Evangelists, better known as *Amsterdam '86*, sponsored once again by the Billy Graham Evangelistic Association. Although the 8,194 evangelists represented a multitude of people groups from 173 nations, a spirit of unity prevailed during the ten-day conference. Just as had happened three years earlier, I was asked to speak on the sensitive subject of personal holiness. I poured my heart out to the evangelists, urging them to walk in purity or risk destroying their ministries. Again, the Holy Spirit worked with power and many settled personal matters with God that night.

Seven team members joined me in Amsterdam, including Dan Owens, who had recently joined our team. A gifted young man, Dan soon became our team's first full-time associate evangelist. The last few years he's also served as emcee for all of our American crusades and greatly assisted with our crusade training and broadcast ministries. I always like to make it clear that Dan doesn't work for me, but with me, as God's evangelist. He's already seen thousands come to Christ through his own ministry of evangelism.

No big breaks

Many seminary students and other enthusiastic young men tell me, "Luis, I want to preach to crowds; I want to be an evangelist and win souls to Christ. How did you get your big break to hold mass crusades?"

There are no big breaks in mass evangelism. I feel God leads in many small ways, and we learn obedience each time. Big doors open on small hinges. If you feel God has called you to serve, be faithful to do everything He shows you to do. Sometimes that means preaching the Gospel to a small group of men behind bars in a state penitentiary. Sometimes that means speaking at the first Parliamentary Prayer Breakfast in Britain's history, which was my privilege that year. You can't do one without doing the other. "He who is faithful in a very little is faithful also in much" (Luke 16:10, RSV).

I often tell young men about the difficulties and warn them to watch out for the four big temptations of pride, immorality, money, and giving up. Whatever we do, God calls us to walk in the light by the power of His Holy Spirit.

Bigger scandals

Unfortunately, several of the biggest names in "televangelism" were strangely absent at *Amsterdam '86*. No one was saying it out loud, but sin was in the camp. A group of secular reporters broke the news about the first big scandal a few months later, during the midst of four weeks of crusades in Fiji and New Zealand in the South Pacific.

Thankfully, a religious writer for one of America's twenty-five largest newspapers had previously spent several weeks doing an in-depth investigation on our ministry. Even though by her own admission she wasn't a Christian, we gave her free rein to examine our audited financial records, interview anyone she wanted, ask any question she wanted, and observe us in action at the office and during one of our crusades. When it was all said and done, Sura Rubenstein knew us almost better than we knew ourselves and wrote a lengthy analysis describing who we were and what we were all about.

When news broke about the Jim and Tammy Bakker scandal in March 1987, this same reporter immediately phoned our office. "Where is Luis?" she asked. "I need to speak to him immediately."

The receptionist politely explained I was out of the country at the moment. "I don't care. I need to speak to Luis. Give me a number where I can reach him."

Half a world away in Fiji, the phone rang. Sura Rubenstein talked with my team member David Jones. She got straight to the point. The scandal that had just erupted could end up tarnishing the reputation of other evangelists, she said, unless we acted quickly. Dave asked what she meant. She explained that she wanted to interview me right then as an excuse to write a big story that night making it clear our team was absolutely above reproach. We'd been praying for Sura's salvation for months, and here she was trying to protect our reputation!

Journalists in New Zealand immediately began clamoring for interviews, as well. I'd already survived a firestorm of controversy that swept New Zealand when four of the nation's leading bishops released a scorching series of accusations about our team's theology, methodology, and motives. Thankfully, their plan backfired and public sentiment swung in our direction! So the New Zealand media actually came to our defense when the Bakker scandal hit.

Revival in New Zealand

Looking back, those were long, hard-driving days of ministry. Four to six daily events drained me of my energy. The voice box practically deserted me, refusing service. There was not a single day's break for four solid weeks.

I poured over the book of the Acts of the Apostles that month. I could identify so closely with the experiences of Peter and Paul and Luke. It was as if a 1,900-year gap didn't stand between us as we saw the Holy Spirit at work!

During that time we rejoiced to see the New York City Marathon women's record-holder, the twenty-one-year-old rebellious daughter of an executive committee member, New Zealand's fifth-ranked professional golfer, the committee-appointed crusade photographer, the prime minister of a South Pacific nation, and 11,426 other people publicly commit their lives to Jesus Christ! Results like that keep one going in the exhausting work of mass evangelism.

That spring I had my first opportunity to preach the Gospel in Africa, leading 350 people to the Lord at a one-night evangelistic rally in Nairobi, Kenya. I also received the first of what would become many invitations to preach the Gospel in communist-dominated Eastern Europe.

That spring our team also received a fantastic church growth report on the results of our Fresno crusade the previous September. A large cross-section of adult decision-makers were interviewed six months after the crusade. Seventy-three percent of the previously "unchurched" inquirers were now actively attending a local church. Even more exciting was the discovery that the 496 decision-makers surveyed reported they already had led another 208 people to Jesus Christ! Here was a documented example of the ongoing evangelism that takes place after every crusade. After all, the most powerful personal witness is a changed life.

Into Eastern Europe

Over Independence Day weekend, it was time for fireworks and family picnics back home. For me, it was time for several tense border crossings, a long drive along unfamiliar roads, and then a warm welcome from Christian brothers I'd never met before behind the Iron Curtain, in Poland—land of Solidarity and some of the greatest reforms experienced by any communist state since World War II. Near one of Poland's most densely populated industrial areas, along its southern border, we held what proved to be the largest evangelistic tent meetings within the Eastern bloc to that point. More than 600 made public commitments to Jesus Christ. Publicly, I stated I felt we were on the verge of seeing God do great things in Eastern Europe. I was thinking of seeing thousands come to Jesus Christ. Little did I know we'd soon see the Iron Curtain fall and personally see more than 101,000 Eastern Europeans commit their lives to the Lord within the next four years!

While in Poland, I visited Auschwitz, where an estimated 4 million died during World War II. What a sobering reminder it was that the issues of life and death and eternity and the sinfulness of fallen man are so much more important than the petty stuff with which we usually concern ourselves in our modern social setting.

35

Twenty-one years after our first evangelistic crusade in Bogota, Colombia, Pat and I were flying home from the city-state of Hong Kong, marveling at what we'd just witnessed. That week we'd preached to packed stadium crowds of up to 45,000 Chinese people at a time. Surprisingly, a number of prominent people crossed the border from the People's Republic of China to see the crusade for themselves. One high-ranking Communist official attended several meetings. He was absolutely astounded that so many people would take a public stand for Jesus Christ and confess God openly. Even more remarkable, a communist college professor came one night and received Christ as Savior on the spot!

We'd seen multiplied thousands come forward in Latin America and Europe, but Pat and I agreed this crusade was our new "benchmark." We'd even seen a tremendous harvest the previous year in Singapore. But nothing like this. In each message, I simply presented the biblical Lord Jesus Christ, stripped of all cultural baggage. The response was amazing. In eight days, more than 31,265 people made first-time or renewed Christian commitments!

Growing international ministry

In many ways, our ministry was becoming more international every day. We had evangelistic rallies and crusades scheduled in eight countries the next year alone.

Ironically, our two most volatile 1988 crusades were back in Mexico, one of the nations I love the most. The Lord helped us overcome the most negative press coverage we'd ever received. We were truly startled by the harshness of the press. We were called "Yankee Imperialists," accused of being CIA agents, and charged with coming to Mexico to "change the customs and culture of the people." I felt like Joseph, who told his brothers in Genesis 50:20— "You intended to harm me, but God intended it for good to accomplish what is now being done, the saving of many lives."

The negative press coverage actually stirred up increased interest in our crusade meetings. At least half of the nearly 100,000 people who attended the meetings had not been attending church. More than 6,140 went forward to publicly commit their lives to Jesus Christ. What's more, we received invitations to come back for additional crusades in Monterrey and the capital city. After two decades, the fields of Mexico were still white unto harvest!

A week before our crusade in Copenhagen, Denmark, that April, we received shocking news. The chairman of the committee that had invited us had just learned he had a massive brain tumor. Within twenty-four hours, he was dead. Yet his dream for the Copenhagen crusade became a tremendous reality. Before his death, he had set three goals for the crusade: a full arena every night, increased unity among the churches in that city, and citywide awareness of the Gospel.

Every night as we watched the 5,500-seat arena fill to capacity, we witnessed our brother's prayers being answered. As we saw 2,500 crusade volunteers from eighty churches and seventeen denominations join together in one united effort to proclaim Christ, we realized his second goal was coming to pass. And when one of Denmark's major television stations aired all six crusade messages the week following the crusade, we knew his third dream had more than come true. The whole country, "Protestant" though it is, was impacted with the message of Jesus Christ!

I wished our brother could have been with us. But the Bible tells us, "There will be more rejoicing in heaven over one sinner who repents than over ninety-nine righteous persons who do not need to repent" (Luke 15:7). Imagine the celebration that took place in heaven as hundreds turned to Christ in Copenhagen that week. And to think our brother was there to join in that celebration!

That summer I spoke at three evangelism leadership conferences back-to-back. The first was the Lausanne-sponsored Leadership '88 conference in Washington, D.C. I challenged the 1,600 young Christian leaders in attendance to make a secret decision in their souls: "Lord Jesus, I'm going to live for Your glory. I will not dishonor Your holy name." Holiness is to be the hallmark of our lives, I pointed out, but we don't need to go around frightened we're going to fall into some gross immorality just because another rash of scandals had surfaced.

In fact, I mentioned I'd stopped saying, "We're all vulnerable—it could happen to anyone." That's not true if we're staying in God's Word, if we're walking by the Spirit, if we're obeying Christ. "If you do these things," 2 Peter 1:10 says, "you will never fall." That's a tremendous promise. If you and I walk in holiness, we will see the power of God at work in our lives. May the Lord keep us and all His servants walking in the light.

The next conference was the International Congress for the Evangelization of the Latin World, in Los Angeles. Some 6,300 leaders from forty nations gathered to discuss working together to reach the entire Spanish-speaking world for Christ. It was a momentous time to meet people who had come to Christ through our ministry in years past, to counsel with some of God's outstanding servant-leaders, to discuss plans for upcoming crusades in Guatemala and Mexico, and to consider invitations for other crusades in Colombia and Spain.

Flying to Washington, D.C., and then to Los Angeles was no problem, but I almost didn't make it to the third conference. Just eight days before leaving, one of my team members received an urgent phone call from Jakarta, Indonesia. One of the conference organizers informed us that I had to obtain a special visa. Normally this isn't required. But because a cult had stirred up problems, Indonesian officials decided to require this visa if someone was coming to their country to speak at a religious conference that could have a "nationwide impact."

News of this visa requirement came as a complete surprise. We immediately took the matter to the Lord, submitted the necessary paperwork, asked many friends and churches to intercede with us, and then waited. A week later, I packed my suitcase . . . wondering if my visa would arrive in time. We were leaving the next morning! But my fellow team members and I were confident God would work out His perfect will.

Just before we had to leave for the Portland International Airport, an express mail courier drove up to our office and hand-delivered my visa. If it had come two hours later, I would have missed my flight and lost the opportunity to minister to nearly 4,000 evangelists, pastors, and other Christian leaders.

The Indonesian government could not have done more to help us and the Lord's hand was clearly evident throughout the conference. We were told that Jakarta '88 was the first opportunity for Indonesia's Christian leaders to gather for a national congress on evangelism. The highlight for me was receiving an invitation to return in a couple of years for large evangelistic "festivals" in Jakarta and two other major cities.

Empty nest

Back home, Pat and I said goodbye to our youngest son, Steve, who was off to play football and start his first year of studies at Wheaton College in Illinois. Growing up playing soccer and practicing all through his high school years had helped Steve develop outstanding skills as a kicker. In less than four years, he would become one of Wheaton's all-time leading scorers.

Even though our four sons were all now young adults, Pat and I previously had made the decision not to empty the nest before it was really empty. We knew Steve deserved the same attention and experiences as our other three sons. So Pat deliberately didn't make any immediate, dramatic changes in her schedule or living situation. True, I was anxious for Pat to travel with me more often. That would happen soon enough. But we wanted Steve to return from college after that first semester and find home still intact.

That fall we held our first evangelistic crusade in Brazil, South America's largest nation. Many people are surprised to learn it's not a Spanish-speaking country, even though Portuguese closely resembles Spanish. Many words are almost identical, although one soon discovers they don't always have exactly the same meaning. So I preached in English, not Spanish, and was glad to have a godly, gifted translator that week.

For seven nights, our live call-in television counseling program aired during prime time in the city of Porto Alegre. Port of Happiness it was not. Earlier in the year, 60 *Minutes* had broadcast a disturbing segment on abused and abandoned Brazilian women and children. On the air, I counseled a woman who had been abandoned by her husband and now relied on prostitution to support her three children. Overwhelmed by guilt, she called to ask for help. Twenty minutes later, as tens of thousands of people watched, she gladly received forgiveness and a new life in Jesus' name. Our crusade team immediately put her in touch with a local church near her home, where she received immediate Christian nurture and practical assistance.

Ever since Keith Bentson and I had prayed for the world when I was a young man, I'd always longed to go to India to preach the pure Gospel. I'd prayed for opportunities to tell Hindus about the uniqueness of God's Son and clearly show that "no one comes to the Father" except through Him. That November, my dream came true during our "Festival of Joy and Hope" in the city of Cuttack in east India.

While we rejoiced to see more than 8,000 come each day to hear the Gospel, demonic activity was almost palpable at times during the festival. On one occasion, I felt either Satan was at work or some of the professing Christians there were secretly living in serious sin. I've seldom had to stop in the middle of my message, as I did then, to address this issue. The result was incredible. The spiritual atmosphere around us was instantly cleared and purified. James 4:7 says, "Resist the devil, and he will flee from you." This was a tremendous victory in an area that has 3,000 Hindu temples.

Hindu influence had so deeply penetrated the state of Orissa, where the city of Cuttack is located, that severe anti-conversion laws are on the books. We weren't surprised, therefore, to find that the number of Christians in the city was perhaps 3,000 maximum. Yet in five days, more than 4,100 made public commitments to Jesus Christ!

The festival marked the first time the churches had invited top government officials to attend a Christian-sponsored activity in that state. The chief minister, a Hindu, participated in the festival's opening ceremonies. He said he had been invited to attend Hindu festivals, a Muslim festival, and now was "glad" that Christians had invited him to their festival. Several other key officials also accepted invitations to attend the evening events in the Cuttack coliseum.

It also was the first time an evangelistic event had been held off church grounds in Orissa. This was important since police officials and local Christian leaders were concerned about possible demonstrations by extremist groups active in that area.

Local television and newspaper reporters provided unprecedented coverage of our Christian festival. In addition, 100,000 homes in Cuttack were visited by volunteers who went door-to-door distributing Scripture portions and festival invitations.

One visitation team, however, was accosted by an extremist group, beaten, and then released. As a precaution, more than 100 policemen were on duty at every festival rally. Yet the Lord turned this around for good. The policemen heard the Gospel clearly presented and several received Christ, including a high-ranking officer!

36

America. As our team geared up to finish the 1980s with a flurry of crusades all over the world, my heart kept turning homeward. I'd studied the rise and fall of Christianity in Western Civilization, and could see this country was in the "transition generation" between the mid-century revival of Christianity and total secularism. One only has to read European history and travel abroad to know the difference between the two is frightening!

In my heart, I felt I could no longer ignore America while seeking to call other nations to Jesus Christ. It wasn't an either/or situation. I felt our team must do both. We'd have to make a lot of changes. Not overnight, of course, but deliberately, strategically, boldly, led by the Spirit of the Lord.

My burden grew all the more when I return to Guatemala where we had yet another fabulous crusade. In a week's time nearly one-quarter million people packed Mateo Flores Stadium to hear the Gospel. When the crowds started overflowing outside the soccer stadium, Pepsi Cola delivery trucks, surrounded by the throngs, used their sound systems to broadcast the crusade music and message. Even people crowded on a nearby hillside could hear the Gospel. More than 6,600 committed their lives to Christ, and another 1,600 had made the same decision at pre-crusade events.

Every Guatemalan Christian I met seemed so proud of the Gospel. They had permeated every sphere of society—politics, education, the military, the business communities, as well as the poorest of the poor. They were planting new churches everywhere. Their commitment was truly impressive and an example, I felt, to westernized Christians who seem to give evangelism only the leftovers instead of their primary attention.

It was obvious the Lord was doing a good work in Guatemala. As that nation's people continued to turn to God, we knew His blessings would follow (Psalm 33:12).

I wanted the same to be true of my adopted homeland, America. I didn't want to make another move, however, before talking to Billy Graham, but for some reason felt nervous about calling him. A couple of weeks later, after reading another report about our ministry, Billy called me in Los Angeles. Where he got my phone number, I don't know.

"Luis," he said, "I just saw that article in *Christianity Today*," talking about our team's multiplicity of crusades. We had just returned from Poland and Hungary, where we'd witnessed unprecedented openness to preach the Gospel. And our team had just accepted invitations to preach the Gospel in what would be the first public stadium evangelistic crusades in the history of the Soviet Union. "Goodness gracious, you're all over the world these days," he exclaimed.

I took a deep breath and said, "Billy, I've got to ask your blessing on something." I explained the burden I'd had, all these years, for America. "I feel the time has come that I should accept more crusade invitations in the States and really go for the bigger cities. But I want to feel that I have your full blessing."

Billy said, "Well, you don't need it. But if you want it, you've got it. Get on with it! Everybody talks about evangelizing America. Now let's really do it."

Of course, he was right. This past generation, from the Vietnam War until now, is massively underevangelized. Far too many Americans nowadays know the language, but they don't know the Lord. As a recent Barna poll so dramatically documented, even a majority of so-called evangelicals have no idea what the pure Gospel is and what it offers.

If I could use only one word to describe the situation in America today, I would say, "Confusion." Top Christian leaders in the past always argued that presence isn't enough. But when critics say "let's stop worrying about America, it's already overevangelized," that's exactly what they're talking about—that the mere presence of Christians means non-Christians have been evangelized. That's an illusion.

According to Gallup, an astounding nine out of ten Americans believe in God. Eight out of ten call themselves "Christians." Four out of ten claim they go to church on any given Sunday. But where is the reality? Where is the witness to a watching world?

Even secular writers were saying it was time for a change. Trend forecasters John Naisbitt and Patricia Aburdene, authors of *Megatrends 2000*, listed "religious revival" as one of ten new directions for the 1990s. And in a *Time* magazine interview, bestselling novelist Tom Wolfe said he, too, expected a religious revival in the '90s. It wasn't a question of "Will there be a revival?" but "What kind will it be?" Unless Christians stepped forward with a clear-cut presentation of the Gospel of Jesus Christ, I feared the New Age gospel of self-improvement would win the day.

Following our eighth successful American crusade in eight years that April, the board of directors mandated that our evangelistic association start to accept invitations for evangelistic crusades in as many as four American metropolitan areas each year.

Ironically, on the heels of that decision, we had promises to keep just about everywhere else the last half of that year. After leading nearly 4,000 people to Jesus Christ during five weeks of crusade meetings all across Wales, our team flew to the Philippines for the Lausanne II in Manila Congress on World Evangelization. There we received twenty-five more invitations for crusades!

Back in Portland about ten days later, while preparing some new evangelistic messages for upcoming crusades, I realized I had two team members in India, another in what was then the Soviet Union, one in Indonesia, one in Colombia, one in Mexico, and many more in regional offices in Argentina, Guatemala, England, and here in the States. The Lord was opening up doors for us left and right. I prayed for wisdom in cutting out anything "extra" from my messages, freeing them from any European/Latin/American cultural baggage.

"War" in Colombia

In the middle of August, several other team members and I said an earnest prayer for safety and then flew to Bogotá, Colombia, following a forty-eight-hour wave of cocaine cartel-ordered political assassinations during which the leading presidential candidate was gunned down in public.

We arrived as the cartel declared "total and absolute war" on the nation. Killings, arson, dynamite blasts, and machine-gun fire made up the top news stories that week. In the midst of one of Colombia's worst crises, I preached to capacity crowds in the capital city. We saw a phenomenal 10,288 people commit their lives to Jesus Christ that week, but the whole crusade almost ended in disaster.

On the closing day, police discovered an arson plot. Thugs had smuggled arson equipment and materials into the 18,000-seat stadium we were using. Apparently the plan was to set the whole thing off during our meeting that Sunday evening. With 23,000 people crammed into the stadium and more than 6,000 crowded outside, the stadium doors and gates were locked during the crusade service. If the fire bomb had gone undetected by the police, a nightmare of catastrophic proportions would have ensued.

As it turned out, the secret service agent assigned to protect me didn't even tell me about the fire bomb scare until the next morning. But the threat was very real in his eyes. When he found out what the police had discovered, he left my side and went straight to his wife, who had come that night with their baby. "There's going to be trouble," he told her. "Go home. I don't want to have to decide between helping you and the man I'm assigned to protect."

Thankfully, the crusade ended without incident—and that secret service agent trusted Christ as Savior. (I met him again not long ago at a Christian conference in Miami. He's gloriously walking with Jesus Christ and boldly serving Him!)

Historic Soviet crusades

While in the Soviet Union a few weeks later for an historic series of crusades in four republics, we received a telegram from Billy Graham that said, "We are praying that God will abundantly bless you and that many people will find Christ. We are praying that your meetings will help open doors for others that may come later." What a wonderful friend and father in Christ Mr. Graham has always been to us! We felt the prayers of God's people every step of the way.

For years I'd dreamed of preaching in cities like Moscow, Leningrad, Kiev, Riga, and Kishinev. But to actually have official government permission to preach the liberating Gospel of Jesus Christ to the masses in Olympic stadiums and other venues—and then to see multiplied thousands come forward—was the thrill of a lifetime!

The Soviet people welcomed us with open arms. One pastor told me the word on the street was, "The only institution in the land with answers is the church." That's it, and they knew it.

I'd never seen so much soul-searching in my life. My interpreter, Viktor Hamm, told me, "People want to confess their sins to God. When you lead them in prayer, say, 'God, forgive my sins. God, forgive my sins.'" Sometimes I'd say it three times, and you could hear the volume go up as people prayed along with us. During each meeting there were moments when people would be suddenly weeping, sobbing, shaking almost uncontrollably. It was a very moving and soul-searching experience, I can tell you.

More than one Soviet Christian leader reminded me, "We don't know what will happen tomorrow." I told the Russian press, "*Glasnost* has spread to mass evangelism. *Perestroika* applies to the restructuring of lives."

After years of fierce repression and violent persecution, the Soviet authorities themselves realized change was in the air. We even received official permission from the highest levels to use the government's own presses to print one million evangelistic booklets. We were elated. Then, at the last minute, a lower level KGB official temporarily blocked our plans to distribute the booklets. Weeks went by. We carried on with another thrilling crusade in Mexico, then returned home, anxious to hear what had happened.

Finally, the roadblock was removed and the one million booklets were finally shipped to all fifteen Soviet republics. Then the world held its breath as communism suddenly collapsed, the Iron Curtain fell overnight, and the Soviet Union disintegrated into a host of separate nations.

The last two weeks of December, it seemed the whole world was glued to the CNN television network, watching the rapidly unfolding events in Eastern Europe and the former Soviet Union and the fall of the Berlin Wall.

That Christmas was our first without the whole family together since our twins were born. Our third son, Andrew, had graduated from the University of Oregon that summer and had moved to Boston to "seek his fortune." In our hearts, Pat and I had unvoiced concerns whether or not he truly intended to walk with the Lord. But there was little we could do now. Andrew was on his own. All we could do was commit him to the Lord, keep the communication lines open, love him, ask God to send someone to cross his path, continue praying, and wait.

37

During 1990 I gained some appreciation for what the apostle Peter must have felt as he preached to a vast multicultural audience of Parthians, Medes, Elamites, Cretans, Arabs, and other visitors gathered in Jerusalem on the day of Pentecost, as described in Acts 2. That year we preached the Gospel of Jesus Christ to Hindus, Buddhists, Muslims, Marxist-Leninist-atheists, Shintoists, pagans, and a goodly number of "Christians" who didn't yet know Christ as Savior. What a challenge!

As we entered the last decade of this millennium, people seemed unusually ready to listen to the message of the Gospel. As Guinness observed, "The world is in a shopping mood for answers." He was absolutely right. Except for the Muslim world and the Christianized West, the world seemed hungry to hear the Good News.

Looking back over church history, I couldn't find any other time with more open doors, with greater possibilities, and with more potential, for evangelism worldwide. Having just experienced an explosive period of evangelism during which we'd seen a record number of people commit their lives to Christ, however, we found Satan opposing us at every turn.

Spiritual warfare

I'd like to tell you that many thousands came to Christ during crusades in cities like Vina Del Mar, Chile; Calcutta, India; and Dhaka, Bangladesh. But each door was shut, most after many months of intense prayer and hard work.

Crusade evangelism is spiritual warfare! The major spiritual battle in every city is to bring the Body of Christ together with the shared conviction that people need the Lord.

Satan, of course, is the great divider. He relishes dividing Christians because it brings dishonor to God and denies His work of reconciliation through the cross of Christ. Look what happened after Pentecost. Satan filled the heart of Ananias to lie to the Holy Spirit and thus cause a disturbance among the believers, who had been one in heart and mind. A short time later, the Grecian Jews in the church started complaining because their widows were not getting as much food as the Hebraic Jewish widows. Again, that was Satan seeking to divide.

The world, the flesh, and the devil—the unholy trinity—are in fierce opposition to the Gospel. Whereas Jesus died to give us life, Satan strives to steal, kill, and destroy (John 10:10). That's why crusade evangelism always has been and always will be spiritual warfare. It gets the spiritual adrenaline flowing.

With several crusades canceled one after another by city officials, natural disasters, and dissension within the Body of Christ, our team looked to the Scriptures. Should we pull back and retreat in defeat? Hardly!

God's Word exhorted us to "Endure hardship . . . like a good soldier of Christ Jesus" (2 Timothy 2:3). We were told to "Be strong in the Lord and in his mighty power. Put on the full armor of God so that you can take your stand against the devil's schemes" (Ephesians 6:10-11). We were reminded that "The weapons we fight with are not the weapons of the world. On the contrary, they have divine power to demolish strongholds" (2 Corinthians 10:4).

From a human point of view, yes, we'd suffered certain setbacks and apparent defeats. But what victories God had in store for us just ahead!

After seeing thousands come to Christ during an evangelistic "festival" in Madras, India, we received an urgent invitation from the newly formed Evangelical Alliance of Romania to come for a series of evangelistic crusades in their newly liberated nation.

Massive revival in Romania

Instead of taking two or three years to make all the necessary preparations, Dr. Paul Negrut and other top Romanian Christian leaders begged us to come that spring. "With the collapse of dictatorship, a vacuum has been created—in politics, in economics, in culture, and especially in the spiritual realm," we were told. "It is absolutely vital that you bring the Gospel of Jesus Christ to our people."

By faith, we said yes, we'd come.

Two days after the nation's first free elections in fifty-three years, we arrived in Romania. A spirit of expectation filled the air. But when 215,000 people jammed three of Romania's largest stadiums over nine days and up to 9,500 came forward *each evening* to commit their lives to Jesus Christ, we were astounded.

"You Romanians are now politically free," I told each audience, "but you can also be spiritually free." Otherwise, my crusade messages were no different from those I'd preached before in many other nations. But the Spirit of God was sweeping across that country with mighty power, convicting people of sin and drawing tens of thousands to the Savior.

Who could believe the miracle happening before our very eyes? It was the book of Acts, Volume II!

That fall we saw 15,000 more people won to Jesus Christ during crusades in Jakarta and Surabaya, Indonesia, and Okinawa and Osaka, Japan. We had a marvelous crusade in Costa Rica that winter, with hundreds of thousands celebrating a century of Gospel proclamation in that nation.

But in our hearts, we couldn't wait to return to Romania for a series of five more crusades the next spring. Decision-makers from the previous year kept coming up to tell us how Christ had revolutionized their lives—from the moment of their conversion. And we literally saw tens of thousands more come to Christ!

In fact, when I gave the invitation on the closing night of our last crusade, in the city of Constanta on the shores of the Black Sea, the crusade chairman and I panicked. Everyone—at first it looked like *everyone*—left his or her seat and came forward. Had they misunderstood?

I explained the basic Gospel message again. "If you've just invited Jesus Christ to come into your life, if you've just accepted God's forgiveness of your sins, raise your hand," I then told the throng gathered in front of the crusade platform.

Virtually everyone lifted a hand!

That evening, 8,200 people made a public declaration of faith in Christ. Nearly eighty percent of the audience! The night before in the same stadium, 8,120 other people had made commitments to Christ.

A journalist asked the crusade chairman, "Is this more than you expected?"

His sparkling eyes and huge smile answered before he spoke in slightly broken English. "Sure!" he said, laughing. "We are just 1,500 evangelicals in Constanta, a town of half a million people. Just four evangelical churches! What a wonderful and blessed time. After forty-five years of communism, it's incredible to see such a deep desire in the heart of so many people to receive Christ."

It was an incredible finale to a fantastic season of harvesting during which more than 85,600 Romanians gave their lives to Christ. The Lausanne Committee reported that well over 1,000 churches were planted!

Time to re-evangelize America

That spring I also had quite a few opportunities to speak here in America, including a keynote address at the National Association of Evangelicals annual convention in St. Louis. I called for a reaffirmation of Christianity's historic belief in the power of Jesus Christ alone to change lives.

"We've got to believe in sudden conversions again," I said. "In the U.S. and Western Europe, we're not sure if Christ has the power to convert people suddenly. That's why we're not seeing as many conversions to Christ. If you present an anemic Christ, who needs a three-year treatment to get you off whatever you're on, that's the kind of Christ people are going to believe in.

"But when we proclaim, 'Christ can change you now. Christ can set you free,' people will respond expecting Him to do just that. That is the power of the living Christ. That is His salvation, and it needs to be known in America."

That spring I also had the opportunity to visit a number of megachurches in several states. I asked each one of the pastors, "What's the secret of your growth?"

The pastor of a church of nearly 4,000, which has also started six other churches in the past thirty years, said, "One word: evangelism."

I asked another pastor, "Why is your church so big?"

He said, "Evangelism. Isn't that the way you're supposed to grow?" Well, yes, it is quite logical! The key to biblical church growth is simple: *Lead people into the kingdom of God* (1 Corinthians 9:22).

That fall the churches of San Antonio, Texas, rejoiced when just over 3,000 were added to the fold in a week. We saw another 17,000 trust Christ during crusades in the capital of Bulgaria, in one of Brazil's leading cities, and in two of the most strategic cities in the Philippines.

Our team's final evangelistic crusade meeting that November was scheduled at Rizal Park in Manila, the capital of the Philippines, at 6:30 p.m. sharp. A cult group had the park reserved that afternoon and was to have dismissed its meeting by five o'clock. But at six they were still there. Doug Steward, our normally reserved senior media producer, boldly walked onto the platform and told them they had to quit!

The tense moment could have turned into a free-for-all. But the cult leaders did clear the platform and even helped our team get everything ready in time for our 6:30 rally. Between 100,000 and 110,000 people filled the park for an evening of Gospel music, testimonies, and the preaching of the true Word of God.

Seeing thousands come to faith in Jesus Christ always is exciting. Dr. Jun Vencer, who soon thereafter became the new general director of the World Evangelical Fellowship, served as chairman for the crusade. He was excited about something else, as well. Working together, we had trained more than 5,000 friendship evangelists, counselors, and follow-up workers. While religious crusades are common in the Philippines, Dr. Vencer told us, "the key difference in this crusade was the massive amount of training. This will be the lasting legacy."

Although I travel just about any other time of the year, Pat can always count on the fact that I'll be home most of December. That Christmas was our thirtieth together as a couple and our first as grandparents.

Absent again, though, was our third son, Andrew, still in Boston working as a manager in a large department store. In my heart I wondered, *How long until he returns to the fold?*

38

I've often made a joke about wanting to live until I'm ninety-two, just like George Müller, but I actually do hope to live that long. If so, I still have several decades left to continue preaching the Gospel with all my heart. While I don't believe in "burning out for God," as spiritual as that might sound, I do believe in burning on for Him with all my heart, soul, and strength.

If there's anything the Church needs today, it's fire—not the short-lived fire of human effort or the flesh, but the mighty fire of the Holy Spirit. As Christians, the Holy Spirit's fire is in us. We must not let that fire die down! Instead, we are to "fan into flame the gift of God, which is in you" (2 Timothy 1:6).

That was my theme during a fast-paced tour throughout the United Kingdom the first part of 1992. While in London, Glasgow, and other cities, I was thrilled to hear many testimonies of those who had trusted the Lord during previous crusades and rallies in England, Scotland, and Wales, and who were still living in the Holy Spirit's indwelling power. Only in Ireland had we yet to hold a major evangelistic crusade, although one was in the works in Dublin later that spring.

New open doors in Mexico

But first it was back to Mexico, where we'd been crusading the past twenty-four years. This time, we had accepted an invitation for three weeklong crusades in the capital city. The best description of those three weeks is found in 1 Corinthians 16:9, where the apostle Paul says, " . . . a great door for effective work has opened to me, and there are many who oppose me."

Mexico's President Carlos Salinas de Gortari indeed opened "a great door" three months earlier when he proposed a series of changes in the nation's constitution, allowing new religious freedoms. I was welcomed to Mexico City as a "distinguished visitor," an honor previously given only twice, we were told, to a religious figure—the Buddhist Nobel Prize winner the Dalai Lama and Pope John Paul II.

But decades of hostility directed at born-again Christians doesn't disappear overnight. Threats of violence and kidnapping, ugly rumors, near cancellation of stadium meetings by midlevel government officials, and the most uninformed, biased press I've ever met tried to stop the advance of the Gospel.

Then, as reported by CNN and *USA Today*, some of the worst smog in world history smothered Mexico City. For two days during the final week of the crusade, emergency measures restricted traffic, shut factories, and canceled classes. Many became sick. Still, crowds of up to 20,000 a night attended our ten crusade meetings in two soccer stadiums and a bullring.

Some government officials and religious leaders expressed alarm that evangelicals were taking advantage of the new religious freedoms too quickly. "Slow down," one official said.

After our last crusade meeting, Mexico City's evangelicals at our urging planned to parade downtown and rally at a national monument there in the capital. Right up until an hour before it began, however, the parade was in jeopardy. Two courageous pastors—one a doctor, the other a lawyer—verbally sparred with midlevel government officials who threatened, "Fine, go ahead and have that parade, but Monday we'll be seeing you."

Hundreds of thousands of Christians filled downtown Mexico City that day, proving the nation's evangelicals were there to stay and were no longer afraid! Never again could they be dismissed as an infinitesimal minority.

In Dublin, Ireland, later that spring, we found born-again Christians there truly *were* a tiny minority, accounting for less than one percent of the capital city's population. The wood of doctrine was there, of course. It just needed the fire of God. "Ireland is one of the most religious countries in the world," I commented on Ireland's top-rated television talk show. "There is an intellectual acceptance of Christianity as a good thing, but many Irish don't have a personal relationship with Jesus Christ"—a theme I repeated throughout the "What's Missing?" campaign.

That summer I spoke at the first of the huge Promise Keepers conferences in Boulder, Colorado. For several years I've been part of a small group of Christian CEOs who meet together weekly for accountability and prayer. But to see tens of thousands of Christian men commit themselves to be godly men of integrity gave me hope for America's spiritual revival. I realized, *God is about to do something great through this movement in our land!*

Then in September, six months after exhilarating crusades in Mexico City, our team crossed the Rio Grande with trepidation. Were Mexico's new religious freedoms taking hold? What sort of welcome would we receive?

Apprehension soon gave way to joy and praise. Reynosa Mayor Ramón Pérez García welcomed us to his city of 750,000 people. On the opening night of our crusade in the Adolfo López Mateos baseball stadium, Mayor Pérez named me guest of honor in front of the near capacity crowd of 14,000. "What energy we have here!" he commented to me.

"It's the energy of God," I suggested.

"Yes, yes," the mayor replied. That night, his wife came forward to receive Christ!

Across the river in McAllen, Texas, area churches united to proclaim the Gospel in a region beset by occult activity, multimillion dollar drug deals, and gang violence. Four rallies in Memorial Stadium drew 32,500 people. *Night Talk*, our live call-in counseling program, aired four nights on the NBC affiliate in Brownsville, pre-empting *The Tonight Show* with Jay Leno. Nine people prayed with me on the air, receiving Jesus Christ as Savior! There in the studio, two cameramen and a control room operator trusted Christ, as well.

All told, more than 5,400 committed their lives to the Lord during our ten days in the Rio Grande Valley. Thousands more were converted during crusades in Panama, Portugal, and Phoenix that fall.

Message to America

At a heavily attended crusade press conference at the America West Arena in Phoenix, NBA Phoenix Suns owner Jerry Colangelo introduced me and I talked about wanting to help bring America back to its days of glory.

How?

First, we have to destroy the spirit of despondency that seems to permeate this nation, I explained. Our currency says, "In God We Trust," but we have gotten away from trusting God. Americans have lost hope.

Second, we need to bring to America an overwhelming spirit of reconciliation. "We've got to get over this business of being hyphenated Americans," I said. "I've been an American for thirty years. My passport doesn't say Hispanic-American. It says citizen of the United States of America." We often use terms like Native American, Afro-American, Italian-American. But the bottom line is, we're all Americans.

Third, we need to restore to America a spirit of holiness. We have lost our sense of embarrassment and shame, our sense of what is proper and honorable and good and right.

Fourth, we need to proclaim forgiveness of sins in Jesus' name. There's an enormous cloud of guilt hanging over most Americans. There's a way to get rid of it, but it's not appearing on "Geraldo" or "Oprah" to confess your sins.

"America needs Good News, not good advice," I stated. "My dream is that people from other nations will look at a revived America and ask, 'What is happening there?' And the answer they will hear: 'A nation has been turned around, and God did it.'"

National crusade in Jamaica

That November Jamaica's Governor-General Sir Howard Cooke, appointed to his position by England's Queen Elizabeth, came out in full support of our upcoming national crusade in his country. He told the media, "We must evangelize the nation or it will perish." Jamaica's largest newspaper turned his statement into a headline, reporting how our crusade could help reverse the moral and spiritual decay facing the country. Among the nation's social ills: epidemic violence and an illegitimate birth rate of more than seventy-five percent.

From north to south and east to west, from parliament to playground, all of Jamaica heard the Gospel three months later. The Governor-general hosted an evangelistic dinner at his official residence, King's House, for instance, that Prime Minister P. J. Patterson, Opposition Party Leader Edward Seaga, and many of the eighty-one members of Jamaica's parliament attended. As I spoke that night, several of the country's top leaders trusted Jesus Christ as Savior.

On the other end of the social spectrum, some 100,000 mostly poor school children in matching uniforms attended a series of more than 100 evangelistic assemblies put on by evangelistic teams from thirteen American churches.

All told, we saw more than 17,500 Jamaicans and one American make first-time or renewed Christian commitments to Jesus Christ. The American was a young man named Andrew Palau, in Jamaica to visit Patricia and me for a few days. After a period of what he calls "some serious repenting," God revolutionized his life.

What a joy to know my son is born of God and bearing the fruit of sonship, being conformed to the likeness of Jesus Christ. What a thrill to see the 180-degree turn Andrew has made. What a delight to sense his enthusiasm for the things of God!

Every child has to make his or her own choices, of course. After Andrew's return to Christ, Pat started to ask him, "Is there anything your father and I could have done to. . . ."

He interrupted, stopping her short. "There's no value in thinking about this," he told her. "Nothing could have stopped me from going my way. I knew what the Bible said. I knew what you and Dad thought. I had a selfish heart and chose to go my own way."

Andrew's passivity to the things of Christ had been a painful, healthy, and sobering lesson to me. Because one of my sons—whom I did my best to channel in the ways of Christ—resisted conversion, I was kept from certain aspects of arrogance and self-righteousness. The Gospel is all of mercy, all of grace.

Yes, I'd had the *privilege* of preaching to vast millions of people and seeing multiplied hundreds of thousands come forward to receive Jesus Christ. But I was not so charming and wonderful as to cause my own son to walk as a saint and never besmirch the name of the Savior. The powerful prayers of God's people and the Lord's anointing when His Word is proclaimed alone bring eternal results.

I now preach the Gospel with ever more conviction. Recently we've had wonderful evangelistic crusades in England, Guatemala, Korea, Poland, Taiwan, and of course the good old United States of America. Many more crusades are just ahead. In fact, we've just accepted invitations for crusades in a couple more of the largest cities in America.

With all my heart, I'm convinced the resurrected Lord Jesus Christ has the power to effect massive positive changes in America, where the vast majority don't live any differently from pagans or atheists, as though God has no claim on their lives. Their hearts have not been transformed, and unless Jesus Christ revolutionizes their hearts, they never will be any different from those outside the Christian faith in foreign lands.

To me, Andrew's conversion is a beautiful picture of what I'd like to see God do for the people of America, young and old. There are thousands of other "Andrews" who need Jesus Christ. My heart goes out to them—and to their families.

Now is the time to re-evangelize this nation!

Correspondence

Thank you for taking the time to read this book. I'd love to hear from you! And I'd be glad to send you our evangelistic team's award-winning ministry newsletter, *LPEA Heartbeat*, free of charge, without any obligation on your part.

It would be an encouragement to know you want to keep in touch and pray for our ongoing ministry—calling America and the nations to Christ. Please write to me today:

Luis Palau
Evangelistic Association
P.O. Box 1173
Portland, OR 97207
U.S.A.

Recommended Reading

Many books have influenced my life and ministry. Below is an abbreviated list of books I've read and reread, marked up, and thoroughly studied over the years. Out of all my library, these are the books that, in case of fire, I'd toss out of the window first, even before my sermon notes and passport.

Spiritual life

The Bible
Authentic Christianity, by Ray C. Stedman
Knowing God, by J. I. Packer
The Liberating Secret, by Norman Grubb
My Utmost for His Highest, by Oswald Chambers
Saving Life of Christ, by Major Ian Thomas

Commentary

The Biblical Expositor, by Carl F. H. Henry, consulting editor
A Commentary, Critical and Explanatory, on the Old and New Testaments, by Robert Jamieson, A. R. Fausset, and David Brown
Ephesians, by August Van Ryn
Hebrews, by S. I. Ridout
Jeremiah, by F. B. Meyer
The New International Bible Commentary, published by Eerdmans
The Pentateuch, by C. H. Mackintosh
Philippians, by F. Lund
Synopsis of the Books of the Bible, by J. N. Darby
Treasury of David, by C. H. Spurgeon

Theology

The Church, by J.B. Watson, editor
The Cross in the New Testament, by Leon Morris
The Cross of Christ, by John Scott
Fundamentalism and the Word of God, by J. I. Packer
Introductory Lectures in Systematic Theology, by Henry C. Thiessen
Revelation and the Bible, by C. F. H. Henry

Practical theology

Divine Plan of Mission, by W. E. Vine

How to Work for Christ, by R . A. Torrey

Lectures to My Students, by C. H. Spurgeon

The Man God Uses, by Oswald J. Smith

The Preacher and His Preaching, by A. F. Gibbs

Spiritual Authority, by Watchman Nee

Whose World, by A. N. Triton

Evangelism and revival

Continuous Revival, by Norman P. Grubb

God in the Garden, by Curtis Mitchell

Mere Christianity, by C. S. Lewis

Missions in Crisis, by Arthur Glassner

Peace with God, by Billy Graham

Revival in Our Time, by William S. Deal

The Revival We Need, by Oswald J. Smith

World Aflame, by Billy Graham

Biography

The Autobiography of Charles G. Finney, by Charles G. Finney and Helen S. Wessel

Billy Graham, by Stanley High

Billy Graham, by John Pollock

The Burning Heart: John Wesley, Evangelist, by A. Skevington Wood

England Before and After Wesley, by J. Wesley Bready

George Whitefield, by John Pollock

George Müller of Bristol, by A. T. Pierson

The Life of D. L. Moody, by William R. Moody

The Memoirs of Robert Murray M'Cheyne, by Robert Murray M'Cheyne

Moody, by J. C. Pollock

Spurgeon—The Early Years—An Autobiography, by C. H. Spurgeon

History

A *History of Christianity*, by Kenneth Scott Latourette
History of the Christian Church, by Philip Schaff
The Making of the President 1960, by Theodore H. White
The Rise and Fall of the Third Reich, by William L. Shirer
The Second World War, by Winston Churchill
The Story of Civilization, by Will Durant
Theology of the English Reformation, by Philip E. Hughes

A Prayer

May the mind of Christ, my Savior,
Live in me from day to day,
By His love and pow'r controlling
All I do and say.

May the Word of God dwell richly
In my heart from hour to hour
So that all may see I triumph
Only thru His pow'r.

May His beauty rest upon me
As I seek the lost to win,
And may they forget the channel,
Seeing only Him.

—*Kate B. Wilkinson*